A Love That Matters

One Family's Journey Through Autism . . . From Heartache to Healing

Diane Vrana

authorHOUSE®

AuthorHouse™
1663 Liberty Drive
Bloomington, IN 47403
www.authorhouse.com
Phone: 1-800-839-8640

First published by AuthorHouse   6/1/2009

ISBN: 978-1-4389-6072-2 (e)
ISBN: 978-1-4389-6071-5 (sc)

Printed in the United States of America
Bloomington, Indiana

This book is printed on acid-free paper.

Disclaimer

The information contained within this book is not intended to diagnose, treat, prevent, or cure any disease, or to provide specific medical advice. Its purpose is to inform, to inspire, and to encourage.

All product and company names mentioned in this book are the properties of the respective organizations. I have no affiliation or monetary involvement with any of the suggested authors or supplemental companies listed. Recommendations are provided solely on personal use and results reached with our child.

Acknowledgments

This book is dedicated with much love and gratitude to the following people and to many others not mentioned. You know who you are.

To my husband, and my best friend, for weathering the storms with me, for loving me more every day, for always believing in me and encouraging me to use my gifts.

To my children, without whom I would not have the richness and ever-filled journey of parenthood! With three boys, let me tell you, there has *never* been a dull moment yet!

To my parents, Floyd (who passed away in August of 2001) and Mary Ann, for instilling in me a core value system of work, faith, family, and tradition, which has helped me to become the parent I am today and has helped me to persevere during our most difficult times.

To my brothers and sisters, for their years of love, laughter, and support; we are truly blessed to be so close and to have one another. I have leaned on them many times, and their support has never faltered.

To the friends I have made along the way—each of you has contributed to who I am today. Thanks to all of you who have laughed, cried, supported, and encouraged me through the more difficult times we've experienced as a family in the last few years. Thank you for your lack of judgment and for your belief in us.

To Mrs. (Peterson) Rude, the best English teacher anyone could have ever asked for! It is because of you that I have felt confident enough to sit down and write a book! And, to Mr. Thomas for always believing and encouraging me, and for never letting me say "I can't."

To Grandma Ann for planting the seed of *doing something* with the information and experiences I've had, for helping me to step out in faith even though I was scared to death! And to Michael for giving me the idea of putting my story into writing, and for giving me a little push now and then to continue on, even when I doubted myself.

To Gerd, our Son-Rise counselor, who helped my family to achieve an awesome at-home therapy program for our son. Gerd, you shared in our setbacks and talked us through our down days, but you also cheered at what may have appeared to others as the smallest of achievements! To our family, those achievements were miraculous and magical, and I feel so blessed to have been able to share them with you. You helped me to learn more about myself, so that I could love my son more fully and be present with him in the moment. You taught me to *dream for more*, but to be *content with what I have today*. I miss our talks, Gerd, and just want you to know that we would never have come as far without your love and guidance. You, and the other teachers and counselors at the Autism Treatment Center of America, are the true heroes of this world. Thank you for being such a blessing to my family, and for helping us to heal our son!

To all of you who may tend to judge that mother who is doing her best to calm a child's tantrum in church or in the grocery store (to all of you who looked at *me* that way), please look at her with love and understanding, rather than with criticism or judgment. Hopefully after reading this book, you will see that there just might be a story behind that tantrum, and you will know for certain that there is a heart behind those tears in her eyes. If you'll just take a moment to look, you will see. Give her and her child your prayers and compassion, not your ignorance or disgust. Thank you—you will have made her world a little more bearable in that moment. You will have given her that little piece of hope and compassion that she so desperately needed that day, that last bit of strength, so that she will be able to continue to be strong for herself and her son or daughter as she continues on her never-ending journey of raising her special needs child.

And I thank all of those who have been closely involved with our journey, for helping us to have faith—faith to believe that things would get better, even though it seemed they never would; faith in a loving God, even though we did not feel very loved at times. I have needed to remind myself that all of this has happened for a *reason,* even if that reason has not been made clear to us quite yet. Perhaps we will not know in this lifetime, but I *do* know that lives have been touched because of Aaren, and lives have been changed, and it is my hope that more lives will be impacted in amazing ways because of our story. God did prevail. He did bring us *healing* through *heartache.*

Preface

Does it matter that I am here to hold you when you cry? Do you even know? My efforts do not seem rewarded; I hold you, and yet you still cry and pull away from me.

Does it matter that I rub your legs each night while you thrash around in your bed? I can feel the knots in your calves, I can see your exhausted face longing for sleep and how you are *just about* to get to that point, when all of a sudden, your little legs start to jerk and thrash about. The peaceful expression on your face turns to a grimace, and a sad and anguished cry escapes your lips. Does it matter that my back is aching after leaning over your crib for so long, that I rub and pray and cry for you?

Does it matter that I have dreams for you? Does it matter that I want you to have your own dreams someday, to live a normal life? Does it matter that I won't accept any less for you, and that I will never stop fighting for you? Does it matter that I would go to the ends of the earth for you—that there isn't anything I would give or do or be to help you? Does it matter that I will die trying to save you?

Does it matter that I lie next to you on the floor and gaze into your eyes when you seem to be in a whole different world, far, far away from me? Does it matter that I whisper "I love you," and "Mommy is here to help you, and I will do everything I can to get you better"? Do my intentions for you matter? Do you hear my vows of love? Does it make any sense to you? I see a fleeting glimmer of recognition run across your face and then watch as it fades into oblivion. Does it matter that I try to reach you in your locked away world?

Does it matter that I spend hours on end with you in your playroom? Sometimes it's as if I may as well be in there by myself. You won't allow me to speak, or sing, hum, or sometimes even to *move*. You can only play with certain toys, and you do not share them all with me, and if I *do* get to play, I need to play them *your* way. Will it always be so? Does it matter that I spend day after day sitting with you like this, with virtually no real results?

Does it matter that I spend night after night on the computer researching your condition and all of the possible treatment options? Will it matter, in the end? Will anything really work, when so many people tell us there is no hope?

Does it matter, God? I think to myself. *Do you see us? Won't you help us? Can't you fix this? Does any of this matter to you?* And as if ushered in through the wind, I feel God say, "Oh, yes, child, it matters. Every intention of love, expressed or withheld, is seen and heard and felt by me, the one who can move mountains for you, the one who can make the sun rise and set, the one who created the stars in the heavens .... Oh, yes, it matters. It does not go unnoticed, and your love for your child will guide your decisions. Your perseverance will make all the difference. Whether I say yes or no is not what is at stake. What matters is the love you have for your child, and the love I have for you." God is love, and ... *love matters.*

Contents

Introduction

"So, Dad, do you want to tell her what you've got?" I heard the doctor ask my husband as I lay on the delivery table for the last time in my life. When my husband was silent for so long, I was sure it was because he was overcome with emotion; we must have had that girl we had longed for, at last! But then I heard him say, "*I'm* not going to tell her. *You'd* better tell her." I was reminded of the old commercial with the little boy named Mikey. "I'm not going to eat it, *you* eat it!" Hmmm… not a good sign. My doctor shouted with joy, "It's a *boy!*" I want to say that I was elated, and that I was ecstatically happy, not caring whether we had a boy or a girl, but that was not the case. A part of me crumbled inside when I heard the news. I had always longed for a girl, even though I loved the two boys we already had at home. I thought *this time* it would be different, I would get that girl. Well, God had other plans for me.

I heard my son cry, and with mixed emotions, I held him for the first time. Oh, yes, there was no doubt I loved him and would love him with everything that I had to give … but a part of me was sad that my dream had died at that moment—my dream of having a girl. And I felt God whisper to me, "*Love is love*," meaning, "It doesn't matter if you have a girl or a boy, your child is *love*." Little did I know that this child would forever change my life—that he would teach me to grow and to learn and to love in ways I could never have imagined. He would bring me closer to God than I had ever been before, and he would virtually rock my world! I was about to embark on a journey that would forever change the way I think, feel, live, and move in this world—a journey that would help me to understand the true meaning of *love*.

It is my hope that as you read this book, not only will you realize that you and your child with autism are *not alone*, but also that this will be a "one-stop shop" for you, in a way. I write this book from my heart and with much personalization, but I also write this book to give you an overview of what autism *is,* signs to look for if you feel your child or someone you know may have the disorder, possible causes and treatments for the disorder, and what resources are out there for you. I know firsthand how overwhelming it can be to be told you have a child with autism and then to go home and feel like, "now what?" Where to start?

There is so much information out there regarding autism, which is a *good thing,* don't get me wrong. But it can feel as if you are spinning in circles with the overwhelming amount of material that is offered. Since I've been right where you are standing at this very moment, it is my desire to share with you the course we took, to offer a "road map," if you will, and to allow you to find your way as we go along. Some of what we tried might appeal to you, and some things might not seem like a good *fit* for your child, and that's okay! My goal is to give you a layout of the path, leaving room for you to veer off in your own direction here and there. Ultimately, I'd like to see us both come back to the final ending point together ... the point of *healing*—for you *and* your child! You can do it! Let's get started!

Chapter 1

What Is Autism, Anyway?

Give me wisdom and knowledge, that I may lead this people,
for who is able to govern this great people of yours?
—2 Chronicles 2:10

They say you can never truly prepare for losing someone you love, no matter how much time you have to do it. I have come to believe that. My dad passed away when I was six months pregnant with my third child, Aaren. He fought a long battle with lung cancer, and even though we did have time to prepare for his leaving us, when that moment finally came, it was so final—so *over*. He was *gone* from our lives, and it was oh so painful. It was a very traumatic time in my life.

At the time, we were also moving into a new house, and it seemed as if life was falling down all around me. My Dad died on August 3, 2001. What I find most interesting and comforting at the same time is that when my third son, Aaren John Vrana was born on a mid-November afternoon, the nurse loudly proclaimed that he was eight pounds, two ounces at birth. Then, she seemed to shout, "*No, wait! He is eight pounds, three ounces. Eight-three!*" she repeated. Those words echoed in my ears, and the meaning resonated in my soul. It was almost as if my dad was trying to get my attention—to let me know he was there. He died on 8-3, and Aaren weighed 8-3. Her words seemed to stand out among the chaos of the busy room, and in that instant, for me, it was as if time stood still. "*Eight-three ...*" Coincidence? I don't believe so. I have no doubt in my mind it

1

was a sign from God letting me know that my dad was there, that he *was* able to see his twentieth grandchild brought into the world. It seemed to complete the circle of life in our family—with the death of a much-loved father, husband, and brother came a new life, a new little man ... my son.

Surely, God had great plans for him; surely there was a reason he gave me another boy, I kept telling myself. God does not make mistakes. So, I watched and waited to see what this new little life in our home would bring. We were about to embark on a journey that we could never have envisioned. We were about to enter the world of *autism* ... a world we had not known existed.

This Thing Called Autism

First, let me begin by stating that there are *two* types of autism: "classic autism," which is autism from birth, and "regressive autism," which, "generally occurs between 12 and 24 months of age after a period of normal development and behavior" (McCandless 2003). Both of these classifications of autism will be discussed in further detail later in this chapter. In both cases, the general symptoms of autism presented, although similar categorically, vary greatly. The behaviors tend to fall "on a spectrum" of variance, which is why autism is considered a "spectrum disorder."

According to the *Diagnostic and Statistical Manual*, 4th Edition, American Psychiatric Association, 1994, to be diagnosed with autistic disorder, at least one sign (each) from parts A, B, and C must be present, plus at least six overall. Those meeting fewer criteria are diagnosable as PDD NOS (Pervasive Development Disorder, Not Otherwise Specified).

A. Qualitative impairments in reciprocal social interaction:

1. Marked impairment in the use of multiple nonverbal behaviors such as eye-to-eye gaze, facial expression, body posture, and gestures to regulate social interaction.
2. Failure to develop peer relationships appropriate to developmental level.

3. Lack of spontaneous seeking to share enjoyment, interests, or achievements with others.
4. Lack of socio-emotional reciprocity.

B. Qualitative impairments in communication:

1. A delay in, or total lack of the development of spoken language (not accompanied by an attempt to compensate through alternative modes of communication such as gesture or mime).
2. Marked impairment in the ability to initiate or sustain a conversation with others despite adequate speech.
3. Stereotyped and repetitive use of language or idiosyncratic language.
4. Lack of varied spontaneous make-believe play or social imitative play appropriate to developmental level.

C. Restricted, repetitive, and stereotyped patterns of behavior, interest, or activity:

1. Encompassing preoccupation with one or more stereotyped and restricted patterns of interest, abnormal either in intensity or focus.
2. An apparently compulsive adherence to specific nonfunctional routines or rituals.
3. Stereotyped and repetitive motor mannerisms (e.g. hand or finger flapping, or twisting, or complex whole body movements).
4. Persistent preoccupation with parts of objects.

Abnormal or impaired development prior to age three manifested by delay or abnormal functioning in at least one of the following areas: (1) social interaction, (2) language as used in social communication, or (3) symbolic or imaginative play.

Okay, that may seem pretty technical. Let's explore this further by looking at a list of characteristics presented by Maria Bird-West Wheeler, an educational and behavioral consultant based in Dallas, Texas, who serves various school districts, educational agencies, and families throughout the nation. She has written the book *Toilet*

Training for Individuals with Autism and Related Disorder, and she co-authored the book, *A Treasure Chest of Behavioral Strategies for Individuals with Autism.* I had the privilege of attending a conference she spoke at in 2007, titled "Behavior and Inclusion on the Autism Spectrum." Ms. Bird-West Wheeler believes that "intervention plans need to include a combination of effective communication supports, sensory calming and sensory development strategies, as well as social skills teaching." Here are the characteristics of autism that she concentrates on when working with children and educators:

❖ **Under- or over-sensitivity to sensory stimuli**
  *sights   *sounds   *odors   *tastes
  *textures   *movement   *people   *emotions
  *demands/commands   *tasks
❖ **High levels of anxiety/intensive emotionality**
  *mental preparation time   *order   *reassurance
❖ **A tendency to respond to stress by developing systems of protection**
  *withdrawal   *avoidance   *aggression
❖ **Neurobehavioral disturbances**
  *disorganized   *distractible   *disorientated
  *inconsistent responses to auditory stimuli
  *tendencies to focus on irrelevant details (could be visual, auditory, smell, etc.)
  *learning style differences
❖ **Poor understanding of nonverbal social cues**
  *body language   *voice pitch, tone, inflection, and loudness
  *facial expression   *eye contact, gaze, gaze shift
❖ **Verbal language difficulties**
  *nonexistent/nonverbal   *literal interpretation
  *use of words without attaching meaning
❖ **Motor planning problems**
  *compliance   *performance   *talking   *handwriting
❖ **Routine and ritualization are of primary importance**
  *predictability   *comfort   *no unexpected surprises

If you believe your child displays any of the above symptoms or meets the criteria for having some form of ASD (Autism Spectrum Disorder), you have come to the right place. You have found your "soft place to fall," as Dr. Phil would say. You are not alone, and there *is* hope for you and your child. In your quest for knowledge, I pray that God will guide your steps and give you the "nuggets" from this book that you can walk away with—the pieces of information that were meant *just for you*.

Classic Autism

The condition "*classic autism*," originally referred to as "*Kanner's Syndrome*," was named after Leo Kanner. Kanner was an MD from Berlin, Germany, who published his first paper identifying autistic children in 1943, asserting he had noticed such children since 1938 (Kanner, 1943). In "classic autism," as stated earlier in this chapter, behaviors in children are noted *from birth*.

Before Kanner noticed and recorded a pattern of symptoms, such children would be classified as emotionally disturbed or mentally retarded. Kanner observed that these children often demonstrated capabilities that showed that they were not merely slow learners, yet they didn't fit the patterns of emotionally disturbed children. Thus he invented a new category, which he called Early Infantile Autism, which has since sometimes been called Kanner's Syndrome. Note that before Kanner incorporated it into his label, the word "autism" already had a meaning: "escape from reality" (coined by Eugen Bleuler in 1912, who had already coined the term "schizophrenia"). Kanner borrowed Bleuler's term either because Kanner indeed believed the children were trying to escape from reality, or he felt that whatever was going on, the children gave that impression (Wobus 1993).

In his 1943 paper, Leo Kanner called attention to what appeared to him as a "*lack of warmth among the fathers and mothers of autistic children*" (Kanner, 1943). In a 1949 paper, he suggested autism may be related to a "genuine lack of maternal warmth," noted that fathers rarely stepped down to indulge in children's play, and observed that children were exposed from "the beginning to parental coldness, obsessiveness, and a mechanical type of attention to material needs only …. They were left neatly in refrigerators which did not defrost. Their withdrawal seems to be an act of turning away from such a situation to seek comfort in solitude" (Kanner 1949).

An article on Wikipedia titled "Refrigerator Mothers," further explains the implications of the "refrigerator mother" as such:

> In the absence of any biomedical explanation for what causes autism after the telltale symptoms were first described by scientists, Bruno Bettelheim, a University of Chicago Professor and child development specialist, and other leading psychoanalysts championed the notion that autism was the product of mothers who were cold, distant and rejecting, thus deprived of the chance to "bond properly." These mothers were often blamed for their children's atypical behaviors, which included rigid rituals, speech difficulty, and self-isolation. As a result, many mothers of autistic children suffered from blame, guilt, and self-doubt from the 1950s throughout the 1970s and beyond: when the prevailing medical belief that autism resulted from inadequate parenting was widely assumed to be correct (Wikipedia, 2008).

Thank goodness this theory has been proven inaccurate in all aspects of the disorder. In fact, in 1964, Bernard Rimland, a psychologist whose son had autism, attacked this theory when he wrote the book, *Infantile Autism: The Syndrome and its Implications for a Neural Theory of Behavior*. However, because children with autism often look like any other child and do not possess physical differences in appearance (unless accompanied by another diagnosis such as Down's syndrome or some such disorder), parents and children are still oftentimes found the object of ridicule by family, friends, and strangers alike. It is my hope that through education of the disorder and awareness by the general public, people will stop jumping to conclusions when observing a child having a tantrum or struggling for self-control.

Raun Kaufman, the son of Barry (Bears) and Samarhia Kaufman, creators of the Son-Rise Therapy Program (see chapter 2), was said to have "classic autism" back in the 1970s. He was also said to have a tested IQ of less than thirty and was considered to be mentally retarded. His parents were told to "concentrate on their other two *healthy* children," and were told to consider "eventual institutionalization" for their young son. Treatments such as electric shock therapy, and tying children to chairs or bedrails were not uncommon in those days. Oftentimes, these children also found themselves placed in the psychiatric ward of a hospital or home and were left to be on their own. Thank goodness science and research of this disorder has helped us to see that these types of treatments are *not* appropriate for children or adults with ASD. Thankfully, we are learning there are so many more things that can be done.

Asperger's Syndrome

At the same time that Kanner was making his observations and assessments of children with these disabilities, a man named Hans Asperger, a doctor of medicine since 1931, raised on a farm just outside of Vienna, Italy, was also pursuing information in this arena. Hans Asperger had a special interest in "psychically abnormal" children. He had written a paper, submitted to the journal in 1943, that was based on investigations of more than four hundred children with "autistic psychopathy" (Schnur, 2005). However, since he traveled little, and all his publishing was in German, until recently Asperger's name was not as well known as that of Leo Kanner. Asperger's Syndrome, which is sometimes referred to as a "high-functioning" form of autism, comes from the works of Hans Asperger. Interestingly, Kanner and Asperger were unaware of one another's work.

Asperger's Syndrome is generally diagnosed during the elementary school years, because the symptoms of the disorder become more apparent at this point. Dr. Paula Kluth, PhD, who also spoke at the conference I attended regarding *Behavior and Inclusion on the Autism Spectrum*, reports symptoms of Asperger's as including variations of the following:

- Poor pragmatic language skills. This phrase means that the child does not use the right tone or volume of voice for a specific context, and does not understand that using humorous or slang expressions also depends on social context.
- Problems with hand-eye coordination and other visual skills.
- Problems making eye contact with others.
- Learning difficulties, which may range from mild to severe.
- Tendency to become absorbed in a particular topic and not know when others are bored with conversations about it. At this stage in their education, children with AS are likely to be labeled as "nerds."
- Repetitive behaviors. These include such behaviors as counting a group of coins or marbles over and over; reciting the same song or poem several times; buttoning and unbuttoning a jacket repeatedly, etc.

You may go to Dr. Kluth's Web site at *paulakluth.com* for more information on ASD disorders, as well as articles and books she has published regarding these issues. Her Web site also consists of a vast array of information regarding strategies and activities to implement an inclusive classroom for children with ASD and other related disorders.

Regressive Autism—Aaren's Diagnosis

Regressive autism, again, as described earlier in this chapter, is autism that develops in a child anywhere between twelve and twenty-four months of age, after a period of *normal development and behavior*. This is the kind of autism our son, Aaren, suffered from. He had started out as a very healthy newborn baby. We took him home from the hospital on that cold, mid-November day, to a home filled with two other rambunctious brothers, a black lab named Gracie, and a large extended family anxious to see the newest addition to our family.

Aaren ate and slept like any newborn, and grew and cooed along with the best of them. He giggled, crawled, played peek-a-boo, and got into mischief, just as any infant/toddler would do. He met every milestone right on time, all within the normal ranges, and I even remember thinking to myself how lucky we were. By about eight or nine months of age, he was already using language and simple words or gestures like "ma-ma," "da-da," and would wave "bye-bye." When put on a slide he would squeal, "Go!" with glee, until we gave him a push down. It was a relief to me, because our middle son was such a late talker, and I remember feeling thankful that Aaren would not have any speech delays or problems. Things seemed to be clicking right along, except for a few things we began to notice as he neared his first birthday.

"When did he start preferring men over women?" asked my husband one day.

"Isn't that strange?" I wondered. This seemed a bit odd, but my mom said that my sister Kathy used to cry every time she saw a man wearing a *hat* at this age! Babies did weird things. So, we just laughed it off as some silly little idiosyncrasy. And then, too, it seemed that lately—and I couldn't put my finger on when this began, exactly—he had started being very agitated and discontented when we would venture out to the supermarket or to some other social outing where there were other people around. His cheeks became awfully rosy all of a sudden, too. I chalked it up to teething, figured he needed a nap and some Tylenol, and didn't think *too much* of it, although it did seem to be happening more and more lately.

Another thing I noticed, before his first birthday, was that he had become very constipated. We changed from formula to milk around nine or ten months of age, and the doctor assured me that some slight constipation was normal until his body would adjust to the milk. Okay, made sense to me. Still, the constipation didn't seem to go away. Well, then there was his first birthday, when he cried and pulled away, and refused to look into the camera as we tried to take his picture and called his name to get his attention. He seemed very annoyed, very cranky, and nearly impossible to console. It didn't make sense, and I began to wonder what happened to my contented, happy, easygoing baby. I hoped it was just a stage or a phase, but unfortunately, this was not to be the case.

His behavior became increasingly difficult over the next few months. We tried to take a family vacation, but by this time, Aaren was virtually incapable of going out in public at all. We hadn't realized this fully until we attempted to take him to an underground aquarium. His brothers thought it was very interesting, but Aaren was terrified of the whole experience. I ended up leaving with him and waiting outside for the family to complete the tour without us.

We tried to go to an outdoor parade, which was overwhelming for him, and then when we had to wait in line to see a display inside a building downtown, we realized that something just was not right with him. He could not stand to be around so many people, he could not stand to have people looking at him, and he fell to the ground and screamed in terror—not just a normal tantrum, mind you, but a blood-curdling scream that echoed throughout the corridor. Embarrassed, sweaty, confused, and fearful of this extreme behavior, I, again, took him outside to wait alone for the rest of the family. Something was not right, and we just didn't know what, and we didn't understand why this was happening. We didn't know then that he was suffering from a disorder called regressive autism—that our happy, contented, and loving baby was becoming a sensory-overloaded, discontented, brain-starved, locked-away child who would need every ounce of energy and time we could devote to him.

Chapter 2

Surrender Is a Choice

*Going a little further, He fell to the ground and prayed
that if possible, the hour might pass from Him. "Abba, Father,"
He said, "everything is possible for you. Take this cup from
Me—yet not what I will, but what You will."*

— Mark 14:35–36

Our Own Rain Man?

"Is he always like this?" was the question I was being asked by a speech therapist from our local school district who had come to my home to take a look at Aaren and assess why he might not be talking yet, even though he was sixteen months old.

"Well, yes, actually, but usually only when people are around," I replied. "It's not always this bad," I said, trying to downplay the way Aaren was screaming and thrashing around on the floor, scooting backward in a fit of terror until he would slide into the wall, bumping his head on the baseboard. I would try to console him, to pick him up, to whisper words of endearment and comfort to him, but to no avail. He could not be comforted, he did not want to be touched, he did not want others looking at him, he could not tolerate other people in his space, and he couldn't talk, so he couldn't tell me what I could do to help him. What was wrong with my child? What had happened to my content little infant? When did all of this begin? It was hard for me to trace this behavior back to a specific time, to a specific situation—it seemed to have come on gradually, slowly, but

11

surely, like a shark, just *lurking* near the surface of the water, waiting to attack. And attack it did—with full force.

Aaren had seemed to develop very normally at first. He was a normal infant, crying only when he was tired or wanted to eat. There was nothing out of the ordinary that would have led us to believe there would be anything wrong with him. He met all of his milestones in his first year, right on target. He cooed, smiled, rolled over, made eye contact, imitated others, played with us, and began to use words. He did it all. It wasn't until he was eight or nine months old that we started to notice some discontent with him at times. He did seem to become more agitated than normal, and more often than normal, at times. For instance, all of a sudden, it seemed that I couldn't take him to the grocery store or some such outing without him making some sort of a major fuss. I chalked it up to "teething" and would bring him home and put him down for a nice long nap after he'd had something to eat. And then there was the fact that he had said his first words and then just seemed to stop talking altogether. That did seem odd, but it happened so gradually that I barely noticed. And in a house with two older brothers, many people told me that his brothers were probably talking for him and that it was very common for a younger child to not use his words if his siblings were getting him what he wanted before he asked for it. The doctor said not to worry and that boys sometimes took longer to talk than girls … so I didn't worry. At first.

Now, though, sitting on the living room floor trying to calm my screaming child, the words of the speech therapist hit me like a loud clap of thunder. "I think we should do more tests …" Tests on *what?* I thought. I know he isn't talking, so can't you just help me to help him talk? What do you mean he needs the "team" out to evaluate him? What *team*, exactly? I began to wonder if I should have ever contacted these people in the first place; look how their presence was traumatizing my son! I should have just left well enough alone, I thought. Little did I know how grateful I would become to the people who first gave me their educated guess that our son had autism. It was a word that frightened me to the core, one that I didn't fully understand. The only image that came to mind was that of *Rain Man*, a movie I had seen starring Tom Cruise and Dustin Hoffman. This was to be our son? We were going to have a *Rain Man?*

The Day of the Diagnosis

"What words does he use?" asked the developmental pediatrician some months later.

"Well," I said, trying to rack my brain to remember the last time he had spoken. "He doesn't really talk anymore, but he used to say quite a few words. Now, he just tends to cry and scream, and honestly, I don't remember the last time I heard him utter a real word."

"How are his bowel movements?" asked the doctor.

"Oh," I said, "that is a whole other problem. He is extremely constipated and has been for a long time. We've tried several different types of medications over the counter and from our pediatrician, but none of them seem to be helping. He still has a hard time with milk and has become a very picky eater and basically eats the same four or five things over and over again. He won't take vitamins and doesn't eat meat of any kind. He won't eat vegetables of any kind, either, and the only fruit he will eat are canned pears and peaches. I was a picky eater as a child, so I assume he takes after me, although even I was a better eater than him."

"How is he sleeping?" the doctor inquired.

"Ha!" I said. "I don't remember the last time either of us had a decent night's sleep. He is tired, I know he is, and he usually falls asleep okay, but he wakes in the night several times. I don't think he's waking to be naughty, either. He seems to be in pain and is kicking his legs and thrashing around in his crib. I try to pick him up, sometimes, but he just arches his back and tries to pull away from me. I try to rock him, but this only makes things worse. When I put him back in his crib, he cries, still, and continues to kick his legs around, as if in pain. The only thing that helps, somewhat, is if I lean over his crib and rub his calf muscles, which seem to be so tight and knotted up. I can see the relief on his face, and he almost falls back to sleep instantly, but as soon as I stop rubbing, he starts thrashing again, and soon is screaming and crying again. We are exhausted, to say the least."

"Hmmm," said the doctor. "I see. How is he with other children?" he asked.

"Well, we've basically stopped being around other people with him altogether, when at all possible, because he cannot tolerate anyone making eye contact with him, talking to him, or being in his space. We cannot go to church, the grocery store, or other people's houses to visit, and we cannot have company over, especially unannounced." As we spoke, my husband had already taken Aaren out of the doctor's office, because he could not tolerate being there. He had screamed and cried when the doctor attempted to speak to him and ended up throwing himself on the floor, banging his head, and giving me a good swat or two, along with a good-sized head butt right to the nose. I was relieved but exhausted when my husband finally did take him out of the office to wait in the car in the parking ramp with him so that I could talk to the doctor in peace.

I explained to the doctor that there was no way I could attempt to go to doctor's visits with Aaren by myself anymore, because he would scream and throw himself down from the minute we walked into a waiting room. The minute I would talk to the receptionist, he would scream so loudly that we could not hear one another, and there was no way to console him or distract him with toys or snacks like I had always been able to do with my other children. Holding him was a virtual wrestling match, because he didn't want to be held or consoled, but I couldn't allow him to scream and kick on the floor, either. So many times I left an office or a store in tears right along with him. I was so embarrassed, and I also was so sad for him, and so scared for what might be wrong. I just didn't understand any of this. Where was my baby?

I left that doctor's appointment with a heavy heart, because he had confirmed our worst fears. He had given my son a diagnosis of autism. I could barely see as I got to the car, as my eyes were so filled with tears. I told my husband what the doctor had said, and we rode home in silence, thankful that Aaren had worked himself up so much at the appointment that he was able to sleep all the way home.

My son had autism, the "regressive type." I didn't know there were types. I didn't know much at this point. We were told that he had a pretty moderate case of the disorder and that we should concentrate on teaching him some *life skills*. The doctor told me to continue to have contact with the school district, and to let them know of the official diagnosis so that we could continue to receive services. He also gave me the name of some speech and occupational therapists in our area and of some schools in our area that specialized in helping children with autism and other special needs. These schools, he said, might be able to help him *improve his life skills*. Those words struck me as hard as if he had slapped me across the face. What? *Life skills?* I didn't want him to have *life skills*. I wanted my *son!* I wanted *all* of him! I felt like screaming out, "I want the little boy who used to gaze into my eyes and snuggle in my arms! I want the little boy who giggled and played peek-a-boo with me! I want the little boy who said, 'ma-ma' and reached his arms out for me! I want my son back, and I will not tolerate limiting myself to helping him gain some *life skills*!!" No, that would not do. There had to be another way, but how? We were basically being told that our son would have a very rough road ahead of him and that the outlook didn't look too promising. The school district had deemed him "a puzzle," and one of the "toughest cases" they had seen.

Further testing by not only the team from our school district (which included a special ed teacher, an autistic specialist, a speech therapist, and an occupational therapist) but also by a pediatric neurologist and a developmental pediatrician confirmed the diagnosis. Aaren had autism, and he was considered to have a moderate to severe case of the disorder, including notable anxiety. No one had the answers we so desperately needed and wanted to hear. They just had a diagnosis, and a heartfelt, "We are sorry."

Life as we knew it came crashing down around us like it had never done before. I felt lost in a sea of confusion and betrayal. I felt as if my baby had been taken from me by a thief in the night right under my nose as I slept. I felt like we were in over our heads, and I wasn't quite sure what to do from here. Our son had regressive autism. In my mind, at that moment, I felt like we had just been told he had a terminal illness. Part of me refused to believe this, and yet my heart just knew that something wasn't right. My beautiful baby … engulfed in a world we could not understand.

Coming Home to Autism

Words cannot describe the feelings of helplessness my husband and I felt during the weeks and months that followed. Sheer terror—

constantly—only begins to describe the feelings associated with some of what we were experiencing. Our other sons were already feeling the effects of having a brother with special needs, because the attention seemed to always focus on Aaren, naturally. *He* was the one who was crying, *he* was the one screaming, *he* was the one banging his head, *he* was the one throwing himself on the floor when someone would stop by unexpectedly, *he* was the one thrashing about in the grocery cart until we left the store … *he* was the one who needed all of our attention. Tempers were short, nerves were frazzled, and fear literally gripped our hearts from morning until night.

I felt that I had already been down this road of "special needs" with our oldest son, as he was diagnosed with ADHD and anxiety when he was just seven. We felt like we'd been through the ringer with him, trying to find the right medications and trying to help him stay organized at school, make and keep friends, *calm down,* and not talk back. Then there was the issue of our middle child. He seemed to always be turned on *high* and was very emotional and intense. He was a late talker, too, and we were starting to wonder if all of the kids didn't have some signs of autistic tendencies. We would find out later that our middle son did have ADHD, but it showed itself very differently from the way it showed itself in his older brother, so it took us quite awhile to pinpoint his diagnosis and get supports in place that really helped him. I was *tired* already, *exhausted* from raising these boys I loved dearly but who *wore me out!* I couldn't imagine the long road ahead of us with Aaren. It just seemed like *way* more than I could handle. My husband and I lingered in denial and self-doubt over the next few months, frozen in time, and yet numbly, somehow, getting through each day. Our home sweet home was nothing short of bitter—riddled with fear, anxiety, short tempers, and depression. Something had to give, and give it did.

Wrestling with God

On one of my (now) regular sleepless nights during a hot, humid summer night in Minnesota (yes, it *does* get *hot* in Minnesota!), I found myself crying myself to sleep once again. But on this particular night, sleep wouldn't come. I lay crying and in my mind, I silently called out to God. "Why? Why have you done this to us? Why would you hurt my baby like this? Why, God, why? I don't want this! I refuse! Take it back! It's too hard! Why must our family suffer so? Why can't you give this to someone else? Haven't you given us enough to deal with? I already lost my father to cancer. I have three boys and didn't get that girl. You already gave me plenty to do with the boys I *did* have. Why did you have to do this to Aaren?" And I felt that God said, "*Let go ...*" And I retorted back with, "What? *No!* I will not let go! I do not want this to be happening! I don't agree with your plan! I want something else!" In this way, I continued to "wrestle with God" late into the night, the tears flowing, my heart aching, my head pounding. And I felt as if God was there, silently listening, letting me get it out, and was patiently waiting for me to *let* him comfort me.

Finally, when every last tear had fallen and every shred of energy had escaped me, I stopped fighting. I imagined that there was a thick rope I was holding onto and that God was holding onto the other end. Here I was, tugging and pulling with all of my might to hang onto that rope, to yank it out of his hands, and all the while he was sitting calmly and silently—with a strength that was no match for my own.

Finally, I "let the rope drop," feeling defeated. I "fell to the ground." In my mind, as I picture it now, I would compare this to the scene in the movie from *The Passion of the Christ*, where Jesus had fallen the second time as he carried his cross to be crucified and Mary came running to him, just as she had done when he was a child. At that moment in time, I felt that my life was going in slow motion just as it did in that scene, my body making a thudding sound as it hit the earth, just as Jesus's body had. I felt as if I could not breathe one more breath, I could not think one more thought, I could not move one more muscle on my own. Time stood excruciatingly still.

I cried out to God to *take this* situation and let his will be done. Whatever that might mean for our future and for Aaren's future ... I gave it to him *completely*. As scary as it was, I stared into the face of uncertainty and didn't back down. I *surrendered*. I want to say I felt better. I want to say I felt relief. I want to say the heavens parted and the angels sang at that very moment ... but none of that happened.

17

Instead, my body started to tremble, and I cried even harder than I had before. I became fully broken before the Lord, completely vulnerable, and I virtually gave him one of the most precious things in my possession ... *my son*. I jokingly told him through my tears that he'd better know what he's *doing*, and, that I hoped that Hh had a plan. I should have known not to doubt. His plan was better than anything I could have ever dreamed up on my own. I'm so glad I "let go" that night and opened myself up to follow him.

Soulful Surrender

Life is not always easy, especially during those times when you find yourself face down on the ground. It is then that you have a choice to make. When faced with difficult circumstances, such as a death of a loved one, a diagnosis of autism, or some other situation just as scary and uncertain, it is *hard* to give that over. Our instinct is to *pray* and *pray* and *pray* that it doesn't have to be so, and sometimes we wrestle with God. And we have to understand that it's okay to do that. God wants to hear from us, even if we feel like giving him a "piece of our mind" sometimes! That's not being disobedient or disrespectful; that is being honest. That is giving him our whole hearts, and that is truly what he wants—*all* of us. But if it must be so ... then pray that he's got a plan for you. Know that his plan might not be what you had hoped for. In fact, it might even be what you had *feared*. But always remember, if it is indeed his plan, then it is exactly what is meant to be. It will all work out in the end, for his glory.

You shall be rewarded tenfold. Even if it's not on this side of heaven, your reward will come! Someone told me once, "There is a special place in heaven for the parents of a special needs child." I hung onto that hope through the difficult days. We had plenty of difficult days ahead of us, and there were *plenty* of times that I wanted to rebel against God's ways. For instance, once I found out that Aaren needed to be put on a very strict diet, I instantly wanted to fight it. I didn't *want* to have to do a special diet for Aaren! "What? No casein? No gluten? What will he *eat*? How will I cook? This just isn't possible! I just want him to be *normal!*" Or some days, I'd find that things seemed to be getting worse instead of better. "What? He's regressing again? I thought he was doing so much better—now he's back to doing *this* again? *Why?*" The days when we seemed to take two steps forward and one step back were so grueling. Many times on our journey through the world of Aaren's autism, I found myself wanting to pick that rope up again, to tug as hard as I could against where God was leading us—not fully trusting that he *did* know what he was doing. It certainly didn't appear that he did! But eventually, I would let go of that rope again—mumbling and grumbling a bit, but I followed his way again, and things would seem to straighten out for awhile.

Surrender Is a Choice

Surrender is a choice we make every moment of every day. We must remember that we are human, and sometimes it is just so difficult to not try to control everything around us on our own—on *our* time schedule, in *our* way. Surely we can do a better job than God can, we think to ourselves. Just look at how long he's sat there doing *nothing*! Move it, already! But just like the words to a famous Christian song proclaim, sometimes we need to say, "God, move the mountain, or move *me*." Sometimes we just have to get out of the way and let God do his thing. This is a true form of surrender. Wave your white flag, and let God know you are ready. Just watch and see what he has in store for you.

I'm not saying we can sit back and do nothing; on the contrary! God wants full participation from us, in every way! It is our responsibility to do anything and everything we feel we can in a situation that needs our attention. However, *where we get our inspiration* for our actions makes all the difference in the world. If we blindly go out into the world trying to "do our own thing," we will ultimately fall flat on our faces more times than not. You see, God keeps giving us chances to surrender—and surrender simply means to quiet ourselves amongst the chaos, and listen for direction from him. And then, by all means, get off your chair and *do something!*

I want to say from the day I decided to surrender this situation to God, it was easy thereafter. I'm afraid not! That's when the real work began! Everything didn't just "fall into place" perfectly all of the time, and if it did, I was sure to thank God for it and realize it wasn't just a coincidence. Just because you surrender and your burdens are lifted, it doesn't mean you still don't have some lifting of your own to do. God will take some but not all of the weight. He wants us to carry our own, too, and if we do, we are sure to see great rewards, some big and some little.

We came to appreciate the tiniest of achievements in Aaren, and his recovery didn't happen all at once. I had to *work* and work *hard* to help my son. I had to work with an intensity that I had never experienced before. I had already put all of my time, energy, and attention into "dealing" with Aaren and his behaviors, but now, I at least had a plan of action, and I knew we could only go up from here. I had hit rock bottom, but because of the power of true surrender, I was ready to pull up my boot straps and get back up again. I felt as if I was climbing Mount Everest, all the while holding Aaren in my arms, praying that I wouldn't let him fall, and thankful that God gave me the courage to not let him stay down at the bottom of that mountain by himself. We were going to fight this thing, he and I, with God as our tour guide. I could not have done this without God. I, as a mere human being with human flaws and weaknesses, could not have healed my son of this grappling disorder. I did not walk alone through my darkest hours, "It was then that he carried me."

Chapter 3

Attitude and Beliefs: The Son-Rise Program

Now faith is being sure of what we hope for and certain of what we do not see.

—Hebrews 11:1

"Okay ... autism. I can *do* this," I would tell myself. I felt like I was in high school, again, out on the floor playing volleyball. As the co-captain, I had to show strength, determination, and tenacity, no matter how far we may have gotten behind. We would give it our all in each and every play, we would never give up, and when the final score was revealed, sometimes we would find we had won! And if we hadn't won, we would walk off of the gym floor feeling proud of ourselves, knowing that we had done our absolute best. We gave it everything we had, no regrets. We had done our very best and had pushed ourselves to the outermost core of our being. Well, I needed to apply that same attitude to this situation, and it was even more important than a high school volleyball game. My son's life was on the line, and he depended on me and the choices we would make from here on out. I could not let him down, as the "co-captain" of his team. With every fiber of my being, I would never give up!

Now that I had finally come to terms with the fact that our son had autism, I immediately went into "task mode" and began to research this whole concept of autism spectrum disorder using every venue I could think of. I immediately went to the library and took out any and all books having anything remotely to do with autism. I spent countless hours, night after night, on the computer late into the evening after the kids were asleep, researching, saving files, bookmarking favorite sites, taking notes, and joining listservs with other parents with children with autism. It literally became my whole world aside from trying to just get through the day with the kids, which was sometimes a task all in itself!

I remember it was the spring of 2004 when I first saw a Web site that just looked *too good to be true*. The Web site featured a program called the Son-Rise Program, and it was one of the *first* sites I had found that had a positive spin on the whole idea of autism and the potential outcomes for children diagnosed with the disorder. I will never forget the simple phrase listed at the bottom of the page, which said, "Autism does not have to be a life sentence." Hello? Had they read my mind? Had they been living my life? Because surely that is about what it felt like, like this thing called autism had entered into our home, took over the body of our baby, and wreaked havoc on our whole household! Basic survival was the mission of every day, which in many ways *did* feel like a death sentence. I looked around on the site and kept thinking, "This just can't be. It's got to be a hoax, it's just too good to be true."

I noticed that there was a program offered to parents through the Son-Rise organization that would help train parents to do an at-home therapy program with their child. This training took place in Massachusetts, and there was no price listed, initially, for how much this would all cost. Well, I then dismissed the whole idea of Son-Rise, thinking that you can't believe everything you read on the internet, and these people just probably wanted my money. Plus, I had never flown in my life, and being deathly *afraid* of flying, I was not about to do so now! I'd have to come all the way from Minnesota, and there was just no way on earth I could do such a thing! This seemed like a long shot. And I knew that once I told my husband about my wild idea of us traveling to Massachusetts for something I saw on the Internet, the dollar signs would be flashing in his eyes, and he would refuse immediately and make some joke about me being gullible. So, I let Son-Rise drop, although I did bookmark the page to refer to later, if for no other reason than to be encouraged by what they had to say.

Over the summer, we had more doctors' appointments and just tried to make it through each day as Aaren would scream, cry, tantrum, and bang his head 90 percent of the time. We could no longer take him to stores with us or to church, to a friend's house, or anywhere, really. The most I could do was go for walks in his stroller with him, but even then, we *had* to go the same way every time, and if I tried to veer left instead of right, he would begin to scream and thrash about in his stroller, letting me know that this is *not* the way we have always gone! So, I'd turn the stroller around and go the same way we always went. The crying would cease, and I would at least get a moment of quiet. Only, I wished that my son would be like others his age and would point out the trees, or say, "Look, Mommy! Airplane!" or some such thing. There would be none of that on our walks—just a deafening silence. Every now and then I would stop the stroller and come around to the front of it and bend down to his level and try to point out a bird, or the clouds, or a car that passed. I would say and point, "Look, Aaren! See the bird? Birds say, 'tweet, tweet, tweet.' Can *you* say tweet-tweet like a birdie?" I would get a fleeting glance, and then Aaren would stare straight ahead as if he hadn't even heard me or was completely not interested in what I was trying to teach him. There were no words, there were no songs or giggles or attempts to make conversation. There was only silence, as he would stare past me—not at me, not through me, but beyond me, to a world I could not see or understand. Soon enough, he would become annoyed that we had stopped walking. So, I'd get behind the stroller again, and start walking, and oftentimes, with tears in my eyes, I would silently start praying.

"Here I am, Lord, show me the way ... you see my child, you see what's happening. How can you just stand there and do nothing? Please show me what to do!" I cannot begin to explain the pain that I felt deep inside, knowing that my child was "different." Knowing that we were not connecting, knowing that I didn't really *know* my child—I didn't know if he had a sense of humor, what his favorite color was, if he loved me, or if he wished on stars. I just didn't feel connected to him at all, because for as much as I'd given of myself, I rarely got anything in return from him. He just couldn't find a way to "let me in." I felt so helpless … so hopeless. It hurt way down deep in the pit of my stomach—the kind of hurt that takes your breath away, a hurt that is so overwhelming that you just can't stand to endure the pain. Where was God then, I wondered? Why did he just sit by silently watching me hurt so much, watching my son struggling to live in his own world. Try as I might to be faithful, to be trusting, and to let him show me the way, I found myself feeling very impatient with him, and feeling abandoned at times. If he had a "master plan" for us, I just wished he would reveal it already and get it over with!

To stand the pain one more second did not seem possible at times like these, which should have been happy and simple, joyful times of taking my child for a walk in the summer. Not so when you have a special needs child. And for those who do not live with a special needs child or have not experienced the difference of having a special needs child and a typical child, well, there just really is no way to explain the pain. It just seems so unfair, and it hurts, plain and simple. We are constantly reminded of what our relationship lacks when we go out in public and view other "typical families" doing "typical activities" without a care in the world. These "typical families" with "typical children" do not seem to be aware at all of the subset of us who are watching from afar, with tears in our eyes and an ache in our heart, at what we wish we had, as they seem to have been given. There are a subset of us living among you who many times become the object of your annoyance, the ones who hold up the line in the grocery store, because our children are not listening, cannot tolerate being around people, or think so rigidly that they insist on throwing a huge tantrum over not getting their way. It is our children who are screaming in church or wriggling around on the floor because someone dared to make eye contact with them, or because their shirt is itching them that day, or because their socks don't feel right in their shoes. It is our child you are judging and our parenting style you are questioning, but please know that there is nothing we would rather have than to have our family appear "typical" like yours does.

Well, it was during one of these walks on a bright and sunny day that soon turned dreary for me when Aaren did not respond to my chatting, or my questioning, that I had an inspiration—I believe given to me by God. I began to talk to God, again out of fear and desperation, but this time, I heard something new. He gave me a way to think about this whole situation in a different light … a way to not feel frenzied and rushed into "fixing" Aaren. A new "motto" just sort of came to me, as in James 3:17, "The wisdom that comes from heaven is first of all pure, and full of quiet gentleness." I didn't hear a thunderous voice, or any voice at all, but I knew the thought that instantaneously yet gently occurred in my mind was not of my own. What I "heard" or "felt" went something like this: "I will keep focusing on what I think God can do with Aaren, and nothing will stop me but him. If he stops me, then I will know it is his will, and I will pray for courage and wisdom at that point. Until then, I'm going to believe that Aaren *will* get 100 percent better, because I know *all things are possible* with God." Surely, I knew that all things *were* possible for God—he that created the heavens and the earth, the stars and the moon, surely my problems could be handled by him with ease. As Proverbs 3:25, 26 states, "Be not afraid of sudden fear … For the Lord shall be thy confidence, and shall keep thy foot from being taken." Be not afraid, and let the Lord give me the confidence I myself did not feel, I thought. I can't tell you how freeing that was, or how much weight was lifted from my shoulders at that moment. Sure, I had to remind myself of my motto daily and sometimes hourly, or even minute by minute … but I now had a motto I could cling to, and a God who was not about to let go of my hand.

Beth Moore, a women's ministry leader, speaker, and author, has said, in her Bible Study Series/DVD, *Believing God* (2002) "We have the supernatural ability to BELIEVE God, and to ACT on our belief." This was exactly what my motto allowed me to do. I was able to have faith in the things I could not see, believing that surely it *is* possible. *Nothing* is impossible with God! For some reason, on the way back from my walk, after my big revelation about my new motto, I thought about the Son-Rise program I had seen on the Internet a couple of months back. I couldn't walk fast enough to get back home and get onto the computer to try to find it again. Something about it felt right now, and I felt that I should at least give it one more try. I felt like God was telling me I had given up too quickly on the notion of what Son-Rise had to offer; I felt like he was telling me it was legitimate. There is no doubt in my mind today that I was getting direction from him that day, because the Son-Rise program has changed our lives and was a part of our protocol that helped recover my son. I had to follow my "mommy instinct," as Jenny McCarthy has called it in her book, *Louder Than Words: A Mother's Journey in Healing Autism*. I believe the "mommy instinct" is really God giving you a nudge in the right direction. Son-Rise was definitely the right direction for us.

The Son-Rise Program—Is It Right For Us?

First, let me tell you that I am not in any way licensed to teach the Son-Rise Program officially. I will not attempt to do that here, but I would like to give a general overview and some basic principles that the program follows, so that you can decide if *your* mommy instinct is directing you to use this program. As far as I'm concerned, my son's recovery happened because we decided to target his autism from all sides. The Son-Rise Therapy Program was the main therapy program we used for him for the first year and a half of his recovery. It was the key that opened the door to his soul, and the key that allowed him to open *his* door and come out and play with *us*. We also delved into the biomedical treatment world, which I will cover in a later chapter. We eventually supplemented our Son-Rise at home therapy program with outside speech therapy, occupational therapy, preschool, and finally play dates to further Aaren's recovery process. Autism, unfortunately, does not have one quick fix, and doing just one thing most likely will not bring you the results you were hoping for. Healing your child of autism will take a *lot* of time and effort on your part, but as they say in the Son-Rise Program, your child is an *investment!* Invest in him or her now, and it *will* pay off later!

The way I looked at the situation at that time, our days were nearly unbearable anyway as it was. It took every ounce of energy I could muster just to *get through the day,* so why not put that much energy into something worthwhile? Let me tell you, you will be much more energized and *re-energized* when you begin to see subtle differences and improvements in your child due to your efforts. This will motivate you to keep going, to keep working, to never give up.

But, you need a plan of action, a guidebook, so to speak, on how to go about each day, what to *do* with the day to help bring your child around. At this point, you may just be getting through the day one way or another, but wouldn't it be wonderful if someone could help you structure your day in a way that your child would be stimulated, thus causing proven neurological brain development and re-wiring? Wouldn't it be great to have a day where you might have an hour or two to *yourself* to re-energize, nap, or just get some things done that you never seem to get to; a day where you can honestly feel that you've made some *gain* in your race to heal your child, where you can noticeably see that you've carried them just a *little bit further?* Well, Son-Rise can help you do that, and so much more.

Son-Rise is the structure, the "curriculum" you will use for your child, the loving yet brilliantly profound way to help your child feel comfortable enough to come out of his world and join ours. Son-Rise teaches you to accept your child *wherever he is*, and to realize that he are doing *the best that he can,* and if he could do better, he *would* be doing better! Son-Rise teaches you to *value* your child, to truly love him unconditionally, just as he is, and to dream *big* for him, but to be happy with whatever the end result may be. That's one tall order, and it doesn't come quickly or easily, but it *does* come, I assure you, along with so many other valuable insights and attitudinal adjustments that you never dreamed possible.

The History of Son-Rise

Following is an excerpt from the book, *Son-Rise, The Miracle Continues* (1994), based on the true story of Raun Kaufman, who was diagnosed as having autism at eighteen months of age, and whose parents would not give up on their child.

> Part One of *Son-Rise: The Miracle Continues* is the astonishing and poignant record of Raun Kaufman's development from a lifeless, non-communicative child into an active, loving, and verbal little boy. When he was a year old, Raun began to withdraw from human contact. Oblivious to his surroundings, he appeared

27

deaf and blind, staring silently for hours, examining his fingers, rocking endlessly, totally self-stimulating. The diagnosis—autism. An irreversible condition.

The experts offered little hope, and as the Kaufmans watched their son slipping further and further into his impenetrable shell, they sensed time was critical. They decided to act on their own—crossing a bridge into uncharted territory in what became the adventure of their lives. When the Kaufmans completed their program based on unconditional love and total acceptance, their son showed no traces of his former condition.

Their story is truly amazing and miraculous, as Raun was *cured* of all autistic tendencies and grew to become an extremely successful, social, and "typical" adult. He is a college graduate of Brown University, where he received a degree in biomedical ethics. In fact, at this moment in time, Raun is the president of the Autism Treatment Center of America, in Sheffield, Massachusetts, which is owned and run by Barry and Samariah Kaufman, Raun's parents. Raun's sister, Bryn, and brother-in-law, William, also work at the Autism Treatment Center of America, as teachers and counselors. It is a family-run business, it is *for real*, and they are there to help you. They are, as coined by a woman at a support group I attended once, the "autism whisperers," in my opinion! They really are the experts in the field, I believe, and I am so thankful that we found them when we did.

Our Personal Son-Rise Journey

After following my heart, and listening to that still, small voice inside of myself, I decided to call the toll-free number given to me off of the Son-Rise Web site. I talked with one of the phone consultants there, who was very kind and as I soon found out, was a former Son-Rise parent of a child who had been diagnosed with autism. He told me that he felt that the Son-Rise program had given him his son back, so to speak, and that he and his wife decided to move from their home in Michigan to go work for the Autism Treatment Center in Sheffield, Massachusetts, to sort of "give back" to the world what good fortune was bestowed upon them. The day that I talked with him, he said his wife had dropped off their son at summer camp, and I couldn't imagine my son ever being well enough to do such a thing. But I hoped, and his words encouraged me that it just might be possible

Well, I had plenty of questions, and I was positive that I would have a situation that had to have been harder than he had, or harder than others he had heard from. After all, my son was banging his head and screaming 90 percent of each and every day. My son could not leave the house or have anyone come into our home who was not immediate family. If my son caught someone's eye, he would instantly throw himself back onto the floor and scream and cry—not just a whimper of a cry, but a blood-curdling scream that bore into your soul, a cry of sheer terror. No, surely no one had ever experienced anything quite like we had, I was certain. Well, to my surprise, I was wrong.

My phone consultant assured me that what we were experiencing with our son was *not* abnormal to families who have a child with autism. I threw questions and scenarios at him left and right, and without one ounce of hesitation, he came back with answers or suggestions, all in a loving and non-critical manner. I knew this was the program for us. I felt even more confident of that now. I could *tell* that these people really had the corner on autism. They understood it like no one else had up to this point in our journey, and they were not intimidated by the behaviors my child displayed. They were not discouraged, either, and helped me not to be, as well. After I got off of the phone, I immediately called my husband, and said, "Honey, we're going to Massachusetts! I signed us up, and we are leaving in three weeks!" I didn't know how we would manage it, I didn't know who would watch the kids or where the money would come from to go, but I just knew we had to go, and nothing would stop us. Three weeks later, we drove out of our driveway in Minnesota, headed for Sheffield, Massachusetts.

Within the first hour of our start-up program at the Autism Treatment Center of America, I knew without a doubt we were in the right place. Looking around at the sixty or seventy other sets of parents there for the same reason that we were, I was certain we had done the right thing, chosen the right therapy, chosen the experts of all experts to help us help our son. So many times I had prayed for God to "show me what to do, or show me where to go," and he did not disappoint me. The tears were flowing in the room, tears of moms and dads who could finally breathe a sigh of relief, who were finally being heard and understood, who could finally come to terms with having a child with autism. The teachers at Son-Rise were there to help us mend our broken souls, to look *within* for healing before we could reach *out* to our child. We were challenged in our thinking, in our belief system, and in our general way of being, but in a good way, never, ever in a way that made us uncomfortable or that forced us to think or feel a certain way. We were taught how to love and accept, how to view our child as a "gift," how to see our children as "special" in a truly meaningful way, rather than in a way that may demean them or make them seem as a burden. The program started with *us*, which surprised me, but made perfect sense all at the same time. We cannot be of help to anyone unless we are at peace within ourselves. We had a lot of inner work to do in that first day or two, but it was so cleansing and so remarkable—truly life-changing.

Of course, we were all eager to learn exactly what we were to *do* with our child, how this Son-Rise program *worked*. We wanted the nuts and bolts and were hungry for the information we had come to gather. We were not led astray, for by the time we left, we had more than enough information to begin our program at home, to begin our journey of healing and growth, for us and for our child.

The basic concepts of the Son-Rise program are:

1.   **Son-Rise is a child-centered program.** It is child-centered, because we want the children to feel that they are in control. They *crave* control because it helps them to feel safe. When they feel safe, they feel confident enough to venture out of their shell just a bit, and once they come out of their shell, then they will see *us* and begin to know *us* and begin to interact with *us* and begin to learn about *our*

world and how they fit into it. The ironic thing with the program was that not only was Aaren coming out to meet us in *our* world, but we also found ourselves entering *his* world, and we were beginning to understand him so much more.

Interestingly, we were told that the Son-Rise Program was 99 percent child-centered. What was the other 1percent? Easy. The one rule to the program that leaves no room for debate is that when the child is in the playroom (you are asked to find a room in your home that is free from distractions to be used for your "play room"), he does not come out until the designated time determined beforehand. Sounds a bit like torture at first, doesn't it? Locking your child in a room to play? That doesn't seem very loving if he wants out, does it? I won't lie, I shed my share of tears at first, but once I saw how good it was for him to be in there, how good it was for him to learn to accept this rule, and how he was able to tolerate other people besides just me or our immediate family ... I was sold. You do have to use a little bit of "tough love," but you do it with grace, without judgment and without getting "upset" with them for crying or carrying on.

Dr. Henry Cloud and Dr. John Townsend, authors of the book, *Boundaries With Kids* (1998), touch on this concept when they say, "People can only internalize rules and laws within a grace atmosphere, otherwise they experience rules as something they hate, something that condemns them, or both: The Law brings wrath (Romans 4:15)." We had to consider what was best for Aaren and then with grace and love, stick firmly to the decision at hand. We enforced the rule of staying in the playroom until we deemed appropriate, because we knew that he needed this one-on-one therapy or his progress could be greatly compromised. Of *course* he would rather be out of the room at first, doing what he had always done before, what was *comfortable* for him, what felt safe. But the idea was to help him to enjoy his playroom and the people he interacted with, so that the playroom itself would become a safe and loving environment in which he could change and grow. There was no greater feeling than having a volunteer come to our home to work with Aaren and watch him excitedly run down to the playroom on his own accord. We knew we had done the right thing with enforcing that 1percent rule right up front.

In our program, we had a volunteer or a family member spend two hours in the playroom with Aaren at a time, and then we would relieve that person and send in another volunteer or family member for another two hours. We did our therapy with Aaren in two-hour increments whenever possible. We averaged twenty-five to thirty hours per week of one-on-one therapy for over a year, in total fifteen hundred-plus hours of individualized Son-Rise therapy for Aaren at the time of his "graduation" from the program. Toward the end of the program, we began to supplement his therapy with outside speech and occupational therapies as well, while still running a Son-Rise therapy program for him in our home. I would take the ideas and goals presented to us by his speech and occupational therapist and incorporate that into our program at home, so that he could have certain skills reinforced throughout the week.

People often ask me where we happened to get our volunteers from and how we did that exactly. I tapped into a few different sources for this. First of all, we were lucky enough to have family members who lived close by who were willing to put in a few hours each week. Next, we turned to friends and teenage volunteers from my son's school come in to help. Last, I contacted a couple of local organizations that specialized in placing volunteers into the community where needed. These organizations generally placed volunteers into homes to work with the elderly or the disabled, and they were a bit surprised to get my call, but intrigued as well. We did receive some volunteers through their agencies—free of charge—who came to work with our son. All of our volunteers were so wonderful and loving with Aaren, and he truly built a loving relationship with each of them.

You may be encountered with family or friends who want to help but don't know what to do for you. Working in the playroom with your child would be a wonderful opportunity for them to help. Do not be afraid to ask! Keep in mind, if you have family or friends who don't feel comfortable working with your child in the playroom, you can ask them to volunteer in other ways, such as mowing the lawn, making a meal for your family once a week, doing your grocery shopping, spending time with your other children, etc . The Son-Rise teachers gave us so many good ideas in this area, and they also helped us to realize that many people want to help in some way, they just may not know how. And not everyone is cut out to work with special needs children, and that's okay. Let them help in other ways so that you can have some free time for working on your program, training your volunteers, providing feedback for a volunteer, spending time with your other children, or to take up a hobby you've put aside because there simply wasn't time.

Galatians 6:2 states, "Carry each other's burdens, and in this way you will fulfill the law of Christ." Don't be so filled with pride that you will not allow others to carry your burdens for a short while—don't be afraid to ask for help. Your child needs *you* to be fulfilled, so that you can have the tenacity and the endurance to run a top-notch program for him. Take care of yourself, so that you can take care of him.

2.   **Son-Rise is parent-directed**. It is parent-directed because, as we learned through the Son-Rise program, *who loves a child more than his parents?* Who is going to be more *motivated* than his parents? Who *knows a child* more than his parents? Who is going to know *what will work and what will not work* more than his parents? The program is set up, as we discussed, so that the parents can recruit volunteers and train the volunteers to interact with their child in a beneficial way. I would strongly advise you not to just accept anyone that comes in off of the street but to actually *interview* your volunteers and have a *trial session* with them and your child. Allow them to be together for a short time at first. If you decide that they might be a good match for your child and for the type of program you want to run, you can discuss details of them becoming a part of your program. With this trial session or period, you will see not only how your child responds, but you will also be able to gather feedback from your volunteer. At this time, you can assess whether they would be suitable for the playroom or perhaps more suited for another task, such as the ones we discussed earlier (mowing the lawn, baking, etc).

The Autism Treatment Center of America also taught us a wonderful "life strategy" to approach any obstacle or to dig deeper in any situation, using the patented "dialogue process." Just as Jesus taught by using stories, he also used an approach to teaching that involved *asking questions*. Oftentimes, those around him would dig deeper because of the questions he would ask them to consider. He knew that the answer could be found from within, even if they were not aware of it. The dialogue process has a similar approach. In it, the participant is challenged to dig deeper into how he or she is feeling about a certain situation through a series of questions. For every question, there is an answer, and there are no right or wrong answers. When using this process, we can begin to understand why we feel a certain way—based on our belief system—and whether we feel we want to change that belief or if we are comfortable with it. It is important to know if your volunteers are open to the Son-Rise method of non-judgment and acceptance, and if they have the energy and enthusiasm that you are looking for. If they appear to be uncomfortable or make a statement that seems a bit critical, don't just cast them aside, but first start by using the dialogue process with them. They may not even be aware of their statement or belief. If they are open to change, then *great!* You can help them do that. If not, they might not be the right fit for the job.

Oftentimes, your child will pick up on something the volunteer may be feeling, even if he or she is not aware of it. Aaren was *classic* at this, and he could always tell, even with me, if I was feeling annoyed, embarrassed, or fearful of his autism or his behavior. Even though I thought I was covering it with a smile or a kind word, deep down, if I wasn't comfortable with his behavior, he could tell. He would react, and once I learned to look a little deeper into myself, I would find the root of my discomfort and talk it through with my husband or a friend/family member, until I was *really* okay with whatever it was that was bothering me. This, we discovered, was a critical piece of the Son-Rise program.

I made it a habit to prepare myself before I went into the playroom with him, and I encouraged our volunteers to do the same. On the outside of the door, I had a picture of him, and alongside the picture, I had two quotes. One was based on the scripture Hebrews 11:1 that leads this chapter, "Now faith is being sure of what we hope for, and certain of what we do not see," and the other was a quote by Robert Frost, "Two roads diverged in a wood and I, I took the road less traveled by, and that has made all the difference." Maybe

Son-Rise was the road less traveled by, but for us, it did make *all* of the difference.

It is important that your volunteers prepare themselves in whatever way is helpful to them before going in to work with your child. Sometimes they will need you to do a dialogue with them to help them clear their path of discomfort, and sometimes it just might not be a good fit. Either way, don't hesitate to take the time to find out before you just put anyone in the playroom with your child. Also, if volunteers aren't comfortable being in the playroom—even though they thought they would be—and they really want to help ... then again, go back to the suggestion listed earlier and ask them if there is anything else they might be interested in doing that could lighten the load for your family.

3.   **Son-Rise is profoundly respectful of the child**. It is a program that sincerely and enthusiastically praises the child for the smallest of achievements. It is a program that values the child and respects where he is coming from, how hard he is working, and that he is doing the best he can. We really did learn to value some of the things that Aaren did, even if we didn't understand them. Paula Kluth (2007) put it well when she spoke at a seminar I attended, based on her book, *You're Going to Love this Kid!" Educating Students with Autism in the Inclusive Classroom*, when she said, "You don't have to *understand* it to *honor* it!" We became like private investigators and began to morph into Aaren's existence when we would join him in his repetitive behaviors. We really began to feel what he felt and see what he saw. We slowly began to understand, at least in part.

A perfect example of this took place during an experience I had with him when we were out of the playroom one time, early on in the program. I had learned the technique of joining, and as we walked down our cul-de-sac on a warm fall day, rather than cringe when he would stop at every green mailbox (the green mailboxes in our area are for a certain paper that some people receive) and rock back and forth while looking at it, I did what I had been trained to do. I joined him. Lovingly, and without judgment, I got right down on his level, stood in front of the first green mailbox, and rocked back and forth. I did this as long as he did, and when he was ready to continue on down the road, I, too, got up and continued to walk. I took note that he chose to pass the houses that did not have a green mailbox, and I walked on alongside him. For some reason, he didn't care to stop at the black mailboxes, I wasn't sure *why*, but I followed his lead.

Well, by the third or fourth green mailbox, as I stood there beside him rocking back and forth, it hit me. I knew why he was stopping at the green mailboxes, and I also knew why he was rocking! The green mailboxes had white lettering on the outside of them, stating the name of the paper that was delivered to that box. If you stood at a certain angle, you could see the letters on the outside of the box, and then when you rocked, if the sun was shining just right, the letters would reflect *inside* of the box. You could see it from both sides in the sun, but the black mailboxes were too dark and not as reflective, so you didn't get the same effect from them. *That* is why he stopped only at the green ones, and *that* is why he moved back and forth! Aha!

I can honestly tell you that this was one of the first times I truly felt connected to my son, and he was nearly three years old. Before Son-Rise, when he would do this, I would shrink from embarrassment, hoping no one could see us. I would try to rush him along, get him focused on the trees or the birds, because I just didn't want to him "look autistic." That would mean he *might be* autistic. Son-Rise taught me to love him just as he was, and once I did that and joined him right at that point without having any expectations otherwise, I truly felt like I had taken one small step to his side of the world. I couldn't wait for him to take his first step into mine.

4. **Son-Rise has a very comprehensive and detailed developmental model to use as a basis for teaching and helping the child to excel.** I have read other books that have talked about therapy programs that are "loving" and "non-judgmental," and it has been stated as if that is a bad thing. It has been alluded to that those programs, whether they were talking about Son-Rise or not, I do not know, but that those types of programs were all just "fluff." That those types of programs weren't offering enough of the "nitty gritty" *work* needed to help a child (or adult) with autism to learn anything other than to be loved and accepted. I am here to tell you that Son-Rise has an excellent set of standards to follow, as well as strong and concrete

assessment tools that can be used. Their program focuses first on the main stumbling blocks of autism, which deal with the social aspect of the disorder: eye contact, language, communication, attention span, and physical touch. Once these areas are strong, the child moves onto the areas of self help skills, cognitive learning, gross motor skills, fine motor skills, friendship skills, conversations skills, etc.

Just let me reiterate that Son-Rise is not a simple "play therapy" full of love and fluff. It is a serious, well thought out, well-organized, and extremely well-planned "curriculum" that is flexible in the sense of letting the child lead until a certain point when the child is ready to be challenged—in a positive and enthusiastic way. The bar is always raised in a way that is challenging without being overwhelming or taxing on the child. It is respectful of where he is, of how much he can do at this moment, but it is *never* limiting in any way. Eventually, the goal is that the child has achieved such success that he is able to be challenged more and more in all areas. The child is taught flexibility through various shared experiences, until eventually, the focus of the program moves from one of extreme child-centeredness to one of a more typical style of program that includes turn taking and rule following. These skills are vital in the real world, in the school setting, on a play date, etc.

It is so amazing and rewarding to watch your child grow stronger and stronger in so many areas, until one day, you find that you are telling a child that was nonverbal for the first three and a half years of his life to *stop talking* and go to sleep. Or you tell a child that used to be afraid of leaving the house or having people over, that he will just have to be a little more patient, because the *ten kids he invited over for his birthday party* won't be here for another hour. And someday it may strike you all of a sudden at how thankful you are that your child says, "Mom, I feel angry, I need a hug," instead of screaming and banging his head against the wall in a fit of uncontrollable rage. And best of all, nothing can capture the bliss in your heart at hearing your child say such things as, "You are too beautiful for my eyes, Mommy," as my little poet just said the other day. I never take for granted the "I love you, Mom," that I hear after night-time prayers and tuck-ins at bedtime, and I'll never forget the phrase my son said on his first day of kindergarten, and many days of school thereafter:

"I'll miss you, Mom, but you're in my heart!" There was a time that I didn't know what he felt in his heart, or *if* he felt anything at all. Now I know, and at those special times, I find myself whispering a prayer of thanksgiving to God—for nudging me in the right direction so long ago on that summer day. And I pray that as you are reading this right now, on this date, at this time that you realize that you were meant to pick up this book. This is not an accident or a coincidence. God has a word for *you!*

If you feel that Son-Rise might be something your family wants to consider, I strongly suggest that you make an initial free phone call to get more information. You can contact someone at Son-Rise by logging onto their Web site at www.son-rise.org, or by calling their toll free number at 1-877-SON-RISE. In fact, when I called for my free "twenty-five-minute" phone call as I mentioned earlier, the consultant that took my call spent over an hour with me! He answered my questions, calmed my fears, and filled me with hope, confidence, and a motivation and excitement that I had not felt up until that point. When you call, make sure you ask about their start-up program, or go to their Web site and view an on-line video that describes that program as well as many other services they provide. It doesn't hurt to look, right? And if money is an issue, do not let that stop you. For one thing, the expenses were nowhere near where we thought they would be, and also, scholarships are offered to qualifying families. So, if money is a concern, make sure you mention that in your initial phone call with a certified counselor. They will help you problem solve anything you may need to work through. If God is giving you that nudge in this direction, please don't hesitate to follow through. At the very least it's worth a phone call, and it could be *the decision* that could help bring your child to recovery.

Other Similar Therapeutic Programs That Might Be Right for You

Disclaimer: The following programs are others that may be similar in some ways to the Son-Rise Therapy Program. They are programs I looked into but have not used personally. I list them here for you to peruse, if you are interested in doing so.

1. **The SCERTS Model**: The SCERTS Model is a comprehensive, educational approach and multidisciplinary framework that addresses the core challenges faced by children with autism spectrum disorder (ASD) and related disabilities. The SCERTS Model prioritizes goals and implements practices that focus on enhancing social communication, emotional regulation, and transactional supports for children with ASD and related social-communicative disabilities and their families. **The SCERTS model is:**

- **Child-centered:**
  Each child's individual patterns of strength and needs guide program planning, including selection of goals and strategies.

- **Family-centered:**
  Family members are included as collaborators and partners in all efforts, and plans are developed to support families.

- **Developmentally grounded:**
  The model and its curriculum is based on extensive research on the development of children with and without disabilities.

- **Activity-based:**
  Everyday activities and routines are the primary contexts in which children learn, and in which progress is measured.

- **Relationship-based:**
  The development of trusting and secure relationships with adult partners and other children provides the foundation for enhancing social communication and emotional regulation capacities.

You can learn more about the SCERTS Model by logging onto their Web site at http://www.scerts.com/index.htm.

2. **RDI (Relationship Development Intervention):**
The Goals of RDI

Dr. Steven Gutstein is the creator of the RDI (Relationship Development Intervention) program. The program is parent-centered, and according to the literature, is intended to help lay missing pathways in the brain. The claims made for RDI are extraordinary;

according to the literature, by following the system parents can expect their children to develop:

- Dramatic improvement in meaningful communication,

- Desire and skills to share their experiences with others,

- Genuine curiosity and enthusiasm for other people,

- Ability to adapt easily and "go with the flow,"

- Amazing increase in the initiation of joint attention,

- Powerful improvement in perspective taking and theory of mind,

- Dramatically increased desire to seek out and interact with peers.

You can learn more about RDI by logging onto their Web site at www.rdiconnect.com. Another good Web site that describes RDI well is **http://www.ctfeat.org/rdi_review.htm.**

3. **Floortime**

Floortime, a vital element of the DIR/Floortime model, is a treatment method as well as a philosophy for interacting with children (and adults as well). Floortime involves meeting a child at his current developmental level and building upon his particular set of strengths. Floortime harnesses the power of a child's motivation; following his lead, wooing him with warm but persistent attempts to engage his attention and tuning in to his interests and desires in interactions. Through Floortime, parents, child care providers, teachers, and therapists help children climb the developmental ladder. By entering into a child's world, we can help him or her learn to relate in meaningful, spontaneous, flexible, and warm ways.

You can learn more about Floortime by logging onto their Web site at **http://www.floortime.org/.**

Chapter 4

Our Steps to Physical Healing— Causes of Autism

When he heard this, Jesus said, "This sickness will not end in death. No, it is for God's glory so that God's Son may be glorified through it."
—John 11:4

Understanding the Causes of Autism

When a child is diagnosed with something—be it autism or something else, such as diabetes or even poor eyesight—oftentimes the first thing parents tend to do is say, "He must get this from *your* side!" We always want to know where to place the blame for such things, in a world so riddled with a virtual smorgasbord of diagnoses. A wife might say, for instance, that her son's ADHD comes from her husband's uncle who, after all, was a bit wild and could never sit still. A husband, in turn, might point the finger at his wife's side of the family when a child is diagnosed with depression or anxiety. Good old Aunt Edna was downright loopy without her medication, after all, he might exclaim. We always want to know where to direct the blame, give an explanation for what we've been dealt, and it was no different in our case. *How could our child have autism? Where did this come from? No one on either side of our family had autism; why were we seeing it in our son?* Whether it will help in dealing with the disorder, it is human nature to want to know *why*, and we found that we almost couldn't move forward until we figured that out first, because it weighed so heavily on our hearts and minds. And for us, finding out the *why* of autism actually led us to understand the *how* of autism, which helped us in our plan to *heal* Aaren from it.

Autism currently affects 1 in 150 children in the United States alone (statistics pertaining to regressive autism). In fact, according to the *US News & World Report (2000)*, "One out of every six children in America suffers from problems such as autism, aggression, dyslexia, and attention deficit hyperactivity disorder." The numbers are staggering and cannot be ignored. In order to treat a condition, it does help to understand it. I knew what my son had, and I knew the symptoms of the disorder, but I didn't understand where it came from and why his body started out completely healthy, and then began to deteriorate. I needed to understand what we were dealing with in order to treat it.

Please keep in mind that what I'm about to explore is considered very controversial. I do not claim to be an expert in this area, but I have taken bits and pieces of information I have acquired in my quest for knowledge on this topic, and I certainly have my opinions about the cause of my son's autism, based on the treatment methods we used and the results we achieved due to the use of those treatments. I will get to that later. But I will generally lay before you some potential causes for autism that research suggests and allow you to form your own opinion from there and perhaps give you an idea of how to proceed in healing your child.

Vaccines

Okay, you've heard all the rage of the controversial topic of vaccinating our children. Some people think it's ridiculous to not vaccinate, while others are dead set against it. We were somewhere in between when Aaren was born. I had started to hear the rumblings of the dismal affects of vaccinating children and how it might contribute to something called autism and other types of neurological disorders, but they were really all just words to me at the time. I hadn't known anyone at the time that was affected by this phenomenon, and it seemed silly to doubt my doctor. After all, he was the "specialist" on the matter, right? What did I know? I was *just* a parent. I didn't have the extensive background and training that he did, so I felt a bit reluctant to bring him my concerns at my son's six-month check-up. I think we, as parents, often feel like we should leave things to the "experts," especially when we are treated curtly if we bring up a question to our nurse or doctor. My doctor was very supportive and kind, but unfortunately was uninformed, in my opinion. Based on what I've learned since this time, I believe that my two older sons—both with an ADHD diagnosis—were affected by their vaccinations, as well, just not to the degree that Aaren was.

At the time of Aaren's six-month check-up, I was student-teaching in a kindergarten classroom. Interestingly, we had a severely autistic student who was being evaluated for possible placement in a center-based program, ultimately taking him out of the public school setting. The supervising teacher who visited our school to make the assessment of this particular child talked with me about my then six-month-old and encouraged me *not* to get his six-month vaccinations at our upcoming check-up. She had said that in her line of work, she had met many, many parents with children with autism and other related disorders who are convinced their child was "normal" at birth, and with each vaccination, slowly but surely regressed over time, to the point of no return for some of them, it seemed. She said that these parents described how their child had gotten sick after a vaccination, some with fevers and flu-like symptoms, which then turned into much worse behaviors like aggression, loss of language, seeming to be in their own world, and so much more. Many of these children ended up with a diagnosis of autism, and she urged me to *at the very least* talk to my doctor about it.

Well, our six-month appointment came along, and I did indeed talk to my doctor about all that this woman had shared with me, and he assured me that these cases were *very* rare and that he had not heard of mercury being used in any of the vaccinations, as this woman had informed me. Bravely, I went so far as to have him check even further, and he left the office to do a little research. When he returned, he said, "Everything is fine. There is no mercury in the vaccinations, just a preservative called thimerisol," and again, he assured me that any side effects from these vaccines were very rare and very mild. I still did not feel completely reassured, especially after the urgings of the supervising teacher who was "out in the trenches" every day … yet I felt silly doubting my doctor and certainly didn't want to cause a scene or make this a big deal. In my mind, I tried to comfort myself by telling myself that babies are brought in for vaccines *every day,* and I should stop worrying about this—I was *sure* my child would be like all the others, and he'd be fine. Why, just look at him, I thought. At six months old, he was a picture of health, always happy, smiling, loving, imitating, cooing, giggling, loving life. He would be *fine!* So, I went ahead and said yes to the shots, and the doctor had the nurse return shortly to give them to him.

I can't tell you how many times I've relived that day when my innocent, vibrant, healthy child looked into my eyes with confusion and fear as I helped to hold him down while the nurse gave him his shots. We all know the feeling, like they are saying, "Mom, what are you letting these people *do* to me? I trusted you! Why are they hurting me?" We've all felt the guilt, and if you are like me, we have shed a tear or two right along with them but knew that it was all "for their own good" and so stayed strong *for them.* He trusted me to take care of him, and I thought I was. We are told that our children need these vaccines so that we will protect them from deadly diseases, but autism, in a way, did bring about the death of that six-month-old child I held in my arms that very day. Within the months to come, and after a couple of more series of vaccines, I had a totally different child in my care, one who did not speak, one who screamed, cried, banged his head, retreated to his own world, would not make eye contact with others, who could not tolerate noises or having people "in his space," who never seemed happy, who seemed fearful and unsure of everyone and everything. Autism had taken the life of my innocent, loving, happy child. And I believe that the thimerisol used in his vaccinations, along with the vaccination schedule used, contributed to his diagnosis of autism. Let me explain a bit about what I've learned about thimerisol.

Thimerisol

So, you say, how is it that something that is supposed to save my child's life from a deadly disease (vaccinations) could actually be harmful to him? Let's first look at the use of *thimerisol*. According to an article in the *Rolling Stone Magazine* posted on June 20, 2005, thimerisol (which is 49.6 percent of ethylmercury by weight) is a mercury-based preservative that "enables the pharmaceutical industry to package vaccines in vials that contain multiple doses, which require additional protection because they are more easily contaminated by multiple needle entries. The larger vials cost half as much to produce as smaller single-dose vials, making it cheaper for international agencies to distribute them to impoverished regions at risk of epidemics." Cost effective? Yes, it would appear so. However, injecting this mercury byproduct into developing infants has proven disastrous.

The article goes on to say, "In 1977, a Russian study found that adults exposed to much lower concentrations of ethylmercury than those given to American children still suffered brain damage years later. Russia banned thimerisol from children's vaccines 20 years ago, and Denmark, Austria, Japan, Great Britain and all the Scandinavian countries have since followed suit" (Kennedy 2005).

Of further interest, reporter Dan Olmsted of UPI decided to head to Lancaster County, Pennsylvania, to find autistic Amish children, if there were any. The Amish do not believe in vaccinating their infant children, and so he decided that if indeed vaccinations did not cause autism, surely he would find autistic children living among the Amish, as in any other subset of population in the United States. According to his calculations, based on the population in Lancaster County, and the percentage of children/adults that should have the disorder, approximately 130 autistic men, women, and children should be living within that community (Olmsted 2005). What he discovered was startling. Olmsted found only four. "One had been exposed to high levels of mercury from a power plant. The other three—including one child adopted from outside the Amish community—had received their vaccines" (Kennedy 2005).

Vaccines containing thimerisol were said to have stopped being made in 2001. However, many of these vaccines remain on clinic shelves, to be "used up" until they are gone. These immunizations do not expire until 2012, so can potentially be used until then. Interestingly, millions of doses of mercury-laden vaccines have been shipped overseas. China, a recipient of many of our vaccines, now has millions of kids with autism. They have a closed gene pool with no history of autism—*ever*. Now they have it. *Do the math*. I always encourage new moms who are getting their children vaccinated to have the doctor or nurse check the insert in any vaccination their child receives, and I also remind them that most of the flu shot vaccines still contain thimerisol as of this writing. For a complete list of vaccines with thimerisol, see the FDA's Web site at http://www. fda.gov/CBER/vaccine/thimerisol.htm#t1.

So, how did thimerisol contribute to the rise in autism? Mercury is a neurotoxin, meaning it affects the nervous system. Mercury poisoning and its effects on humans date back to the nineteenth century. Workers known as "hatters," or those that worked in the hat-making industry, were exposed to mercury in the felt-making process, where mercury was rubbed onto cloth to preserve it. The workers were dubbed the nickname the "mad hatters," because of the neurologically disturbing symptoms they displayed after exposure to the toxin. They were said to have symptoms such as personality changes, sometimes even "insanity," as well as nervousness, "trembling (known as "hatters' shakes"), loss of coordination, slurred speech, loosening of teeth, memory loss, depression, irritability and anxiety" (Connealy 2006).

As McCandless (2002) points out, "Even the 19th Century author, Lewis Carroll knew that mercury was one of the most toxic substances on earth." Carroll "indirectly referred to its dangers through the *Mad Hatter*, his Alice in Wonderland character." But, it is no laughing matter, especially when innocent children are affected. According to McCandless, "Concern about mercury (poisoning) stems from its effects on the brain, nervous system, and the gastrointestinal system." She goes on to say that "mercury poisoning induces cognitive and social deficits, including loss of speech or failure to develop it, memory impairment, poor concentration, word comprehension difficulties, and an assortment of autism-like behaviors including sleep difficulties, self-injurious behavior (e.g., head banging and self-biting) agitation, unprovoked crying, and staring spells." And to think, the government knowingly chose thimerisol as a preservative in the vaccines for our children! It's preposterous!

Interestingly, the *Rolling Stone* article previously mentioned (Kennedy, 2005) also states that during the Second World War, when the department of defense used the preservative in vaccines on soldiers, it required Lilly to label it *poison*. In 1967, according to the article, "A study in *Applied Microbiology* found that thimerisol killed mice when added to injected vaccines." Furthermore, it states, "Four years later, Lilly's own studies discerned that thimerisol was toxic to tissue cells in concentrations as low as one part per million—*100 times weaker than the concentration in a typical vaccine.*" Even with all of this evidence of the harmful effects of thimerisol, the company "continued to promote thimerisol as *'nontoxic'* and also incorporated it into topical disinfectants. In 1977, ten babies at a Toronto hospital died when an antiseptic preserved with thimerisol was dabbed onto their umbilical cords."

Essentially, injected infants and toddlers vaccinated prior to 2001, but not excluding vaccines given after that year, were vulnerable to mercury poisoning. As stated in the *Rolling Stone* article referred to above, "At two months of age, when the infant brain is still at a critical stage of development, infants routinely received three inoculations that contained a total of 62.5 micrograms of ethyl mercury—a level 99 times greater than the EPS's limit for daily exposure to methyl mercury, a related neurotoxin. Although the vaccine industry insists that ethyl mercury poses little danger because it breaks down rapidly and is removed by the body, several studies—including one published in April by the National Institutes of Health—suggest that ethyl mercury is actually MORE toxic to developing brains, and stays in the brain *longer* than methyl mercury." And to think, on top of all of that, newborns are vaccinated with thimerisol-laced vaccine for hepatitis B within twenty-four hours of birth, when their neurological systems are crucially vulnerable! In the first six months of life, infants born between the years of 1989–2001 and beyond got "not one, but three doses of Hepatitis B vaccine and three doses of the thimerisol-containing Hib or Human Influenza B vaccine" (McCandless 2004). McCandless explains that "not counting maternal exposures, for many infants the levels of mercury exceeded the EPA's guidelines for 'safe' exposure *in adults.*"

Immunization Schedule

I do not feel that vaccinations alone are to blame for the rise in autism. I do see merit in using vaccinations, but I would definitely prefer a thimerisol-free version as we had in the past, before the surge of autism began. I also believe that the vaccine schedule should be taken into account. According to research compiled in June of 2008 by a team from the Generation Rescue organization, "In the 1980s, children received 10 vaccines by the age of 5. Today, they receive 36." That is definitely something to consider, in light of the rise in autism and the addition of vaccinations given to our children over the years. The question is posed on the Web site, "Were children dying of these diseases 25 years ago?" The answer is no! So one must ask, why the increase in vaccinations? Below are some recommendations listed on the Generation Rescue Web site regarding the use of vaccinations for your child. For more detailed information, log onto http://www.generationrescue.org/vaccines.html.

Take Precaution

- Consider delaying vaccines until your child is eighteen to twenty-four months old.

- Do not vaccinate if your child is taking antibiotics.

- Consider no more than one vaccine per doctor's visit.

- If you plan to get the MMR vaccine, ask your doctor to give it in three separate vaccines for measles, mumps, and rubella.

- Consider giving high doses of Vitamin C (3,000–5,000 mg per day) on the day before, of, and after vaccination.

- If your child experiences any developmental delays, stop vaccinating until you learn more.

- Always ask to see the vaccine insert, and never accept a vaccine that uses thimerisol. (Most flu shots today still contain thimerisol)

Another article found on that site explains more about spacing out or delaying vaccinations, which vaccinations are really necessary, and how you can go about talking with your doctor about your concerns. The article is titled, *A User-Friendly Vaccine Schedule*, written by University of Washington surgeon Donald Miller, MD, and can be found specifically at http://www.generationrescue.org/pdf/user_friendly.pdf.

I have heard some parents exclaim that they have eliminated the need for "traditional vaccinations" as they have discovered a form of homeopathic alternative to the vaccines. It is definitely an area to explore by talking with a healthcare practitioner who is licensed in the area of homeopathy. For more information on this topic, you can log onto http://www.cure-guide.com or read the book, *The Vaccine Guide: Risks and Benefits for Children and Adults*, by Randall Neustaedter, OMD, LAC.

Candida/Yeast

According to Stephen M. Edelson, PhD, in an article written and posted on the Autism Research Institute Web site (http://www.autism.com/triggers/candida_org.htm), "There is a great deal of evidence that a form of yeast, candida albicans, may cause autism and may exacerbate many behavior and health problems in autistic individuals, especially those with late-onset autism." How does your child get this overload of yeast in his/her body? Oftentimes it is due to repeated doses of antibiotics for ear infections and other such ailments when children are young. Edelson's article explains:

> Candida albicans belongs to the yeast family and is a single-cell fungus. This form of yeast is located in various parts of the body including the digestive tract. Generally speaking, benign microbes limit the amount of yeast in the intestinal tract, and thus, keep the yeast under control. However, exposure to antibiotics, especially repeated exposure, can destroy these microbes. This can result in an overgrowth of candida albicans. When the yeast multiplies, it releases

toxins in the body; and these toxins are known to impair the central nervous system and the immune system.

Some of the behaviors you may see when a child has yeast overgrowth, according to Edelson, are, "Headaches, stomachaches, constipation, gas pains, fatigue, and depression." He goes onto say, "These problems are often worse during damp and/or muggy days and in moldy places," and that "exposure to perfumes and insecticides can worsen the condition." Diane Craft, MA, CNHP, describes other symptoms, such as: poor attention, hyperactivity, anger, mood swings, irritability, "spaciness," inappropriate behavior (such as making odd noises or talking very loudly), and memory problems. Craft goes on to say, "They may also have physical signs of yeast overgrowth that include a distinct 'yeasty' smell, and cravings for foods that yeast thrives on, such as sugars and carbohydrates, as well as a whitish coating of the tongue, diaper rash, and/or itching around the anus."

Dr. William Shaw, PhD, who serves as director of the Great Plains laboratory for health, metabolism, and nutrition in Lenexa, Kansas, has conducted important research on yeast and its effects on autistic individuals. As stated in Edelson's article, Dr. Shaw "recently discovered unusual microbial metabolites in the urine of autistic children who responded remarkably well to anti-fungal treatments. Dr. Shaw and his colleagues observed a decrease in urinary organic acids as well as decreases in hyperactivity and self-stimulatory, stereotyped behavior; and increases in eye contact, vocalization, and concentration." Treating the yeast overgrowth is imperative to improving these types of symptoms. Edelson's article lists some safe suggestions for doing just that, such as, "taking nutritional supplements which replenish the intestinal tract with 'good' microbes (e.g., acidophilus) and/or taking anti-fungal medications (e.g., Nystatin, Ketoconosal, Diflucan)." A special diet low in sugar and other foods on which yeast thrives is also recommended. A book based specifically on this topic is *Breaking the Vicious Cycle*, by Elaine Gottsschall. You may log onto Gottsschall's Web site at http://www.breakingtheviciouscycle.info to get more information, as well as information on her modified diet plan for children and adults being treated with yeast issues, called "The Specific Carbohydrate Diet," or "SCD."

Genetic Precursors and/or Triggers

I have never understood the researchers who claim that autism is hereditary. How could that be when I am not autistic, and my husband is not autistic, and there is no one on either side of our family that is autistic? Is it so simple as to find a gene or a chromosome that is responsible for this? According to an article published in February of 2007 by the NICHD, part of the National Institutes of Health within the U.S. Department of Health and Human Services, "The largest search for autism genes to date (funded in part by the NIH) has implicated components of the brain's glutamate chemical messenger system and a previously overlooked site on chromosome 11. Based on 1,168 families with at least two affected members, the genome scan also adds to evidence that tiny, rare variations in genes may heighten risk for autism spectrum disorders (ASD)."

In a similar article posted in October of 2006, it was said that "A version of a gene has been linked to autism in families that have more than one child with the disorder. Inheriting two copies of this version more than doubled a child's risk of developing an autism spectrum disorder." The article went on to say, "Autism is one of the most heritable mental disorders. If one identical twin has it, so will the other in nearly 9 out of 10 cases. If one sibling has the disorder, the other siblings run a 35-fold greater-than-normal risk of having it. Still, scientists have so far had only mixed success in identifying the genes involved." Furthermore, the article stated, "This common gene variant likely predisposes for autism in combination with other genes and environmental factors." In my research of this topic, it appears that different sources contemplate that there could be up to fifty genes involved, and it could be quite some time before any real answers in this area are found.

Marci Wheeler, a field instructor and adjunct faculty member for the School of Social Work at Indiana University and Indiana University-Purdue summed up the concept nicely when she said, "In the majority of cases, there is likely a complex relationship between a genetic predisposition and an environmental trigger that results in the behavioral symptoms of an autism spectrum disorder diagnosis" (2008).

Simply speaking, there is *no one thing* so far that is believed to cause autism, but rather, a combination of factors. Wheeler goes on to explain that there are "four broad areas of focus which conceptualize the possible biomedical causes of autism spectrum disorders. Most researchers and practioners feel that all four areas are intertwined and that each affects the other." The four areas she describes are: gastrointestinal abnormalities, immune dysfunctions, detoxification abnormalities, and/or nutritional deficiencies or imbalances. Wheeler defined these four areas as such:

1.   Gastrointestinal abnormalities:

For children on the autism spectrum, symptoms of gastrointestinal problems may include; diarrhea, constipation, reflux, food cravings, bloating, fatigue, aggression, sleep difficulties, "spaciness," agitation, inappropriate laughing, and "stim" behaviors, including hand movements, toe walking, and spinning objects or self. Gastrointestinal abnormalities may be due to the following ailments:

- Bacteria, yeast, or fungus overgrowth (Shaw 1998);
- "Leaky gut" defined as increased permeability of the intestinal lining, often caused by chronic inflammation that is often due to yeast and/or the inability to break down proteins from casein (dairy products) and gluten (wheat, barley, rye, oats, and other grains) which then leak into the bloodstream and travel to and impact various tissues, including the brain, possibly causing an opiate effect in the brain (McCandless 2002);
- Alteration of intestinal flora as a result of antibiotic use for common childhood infections such as earaches (Shaw 1998); or
- Enterocolitis; a unique inflammation due to the presence of the measles virus in the intestinal tract: ileal hyperplasia (McCandless 2002).

2.   Immune Dysfunctions:

Signs of impaired immunity in children on the autism spectrum may include: cyclic fevers, compulsive behaviors, skin rashes or eczema, impulsivity, aggression, and bowel problems such as diarrhea, constipation, impaction, and/or blood and mucus in stools. There are also anecdotal stories of children with autism who spike a high fever that results in a dramatic increase in awareness as well as communication and social abilities (Blakeslee 2005). This effect is lost again when the fever subsides. This is thought to relate to differences in the immune system. Immune system dysfunctions are believed to impact brain development or functioning in susceptible individuals.

Immune dysfunction is thought to be a result of the following genetically linked or environmentally acquired ailments:

- Viruses that are present that may or may not be detected according to the symptoms presented (McCandless 2002);
- "Leaky gut" (McCandless 2002);
- Infections treated with antibiotics that over time alter the immune system (Shaw 1998);
- Genetic predisposition to autoimmune diseases in the family (McCandless 2002); or
- Allergies or sensitivities to foods (Marohn 2002).

3.   Detoxification abnormalities

Children on the autism spectrum may show signs of impaired detoxification such as: sensory issues, sleep difficulties, stimming, impulsivity, aggression, compulsive behaviors, night sweats, anxiety, dilated pupils, and lack of speech or pica (ingestion of inedible items). Detoxification abnormalities may be related to a genetically linked susceptibility or an environmentally acquired condition such as the following:

- Methionine cycle abnormalities; part of the body's required sulfation process (James 2005);

- Methylation may be impaired for some individuals; this is a process by which organic chemicals are made available for various important body functions (Marohn 2002);
- Glutathione synthesis abnormalities; glutathione naturally rids the body of heavy metals (James 2005);
- Metallothionein (MT) dysfunction has been seen in some individuals; zinc-copper balance and detoxification of heavy metals are key roles of MT, a protein in the body (McCandless 2002); or
- Oxidative stress; damage caused by build-up of metabolic by-products often due to glutathione depletion (James 2005).

Detoxification abnormalities are thought to contribute to the build-up of heavy metals in the tissues, including the brains of individuals on the autism spectrum. Symptoms of heavy metal exposure are similar to many of the symptoms of autism spectrum disorders.

4.   Nutritional Deficiencies

Nutritional deficiencies or imbalances are a fourth major biomedical area of concern that families and professionals address. Common symptoms of nutritional abnormalities in children on the autism spectrum may include: being underweight or overweight, anxiety, mood swings, sensory issues, lack of speech, stimming, aggression, impulsivity, eye poking, dry hair or skin, and pica (ingestion of inedible items).

Whether nutritional deficiencies and imbalances are a cause of or a result of an autism spectrum disorder is not clear. Nutritional problems can result from malabsorption of nutrients and/or problems with digestion that may be associated with the gastrointestinal, immune, and detoxification problems.

Basically, this is still a confusing and controversial area of understanding, but we *do* know that autism is *not* caused from mothers or fathers not loving their child enough, as was thought so many years ago. So, if you recently discovered that your child has autism and you are sitting there wondering "why?" just know that it isn't anything you *did* or *didn't do*, that it isn't your husband's fault, or your wife's fault, that you aren't to blame for making certain decisions (such as choosing to vaccinate according to the schedule your pediatrician has laid out for you), and that you did the best you could with the information you had. In some cases, you didn't *have* any information, and you know that you would never have chosen to do something to harm your child. Be free of all guilt, let it go ... just take what you can from information now presented to you and learn and grow from there as you continue the journey of healing for your child. You can do it! Let's surge ahead together ....

Chapter 5

Our Steps to Physical Healing— the Biomedical Intervention Process

So Moses cried out to the LORD, "O God, please heal her!"
—Numbers 12:13

Before I even begin delving into this chapter any further, I need to acknowledge a woman I have never met in person but who I feel deserves special recognition, because, unbeknownst to her, she was our "saving grace" in the arena of biomedical intervention for our son. I have mentioned her several times throughout this book already but have not "formally introduced her." The woman's name is Dr. Jaquelyn McCandless, and she is the author of the book, *Children with Starving Brains* and is also a grandmother of a child with autism. It is because of her that I was able to navigate my way through the intricate roadways of healing options and necessities for my son. A heartfelt thank you does not seem adequate for all that her book has done for us. I just want to mention, too, that Dr. McCandless had her own listserv at the time (and possibly still does?), and I would write in, as would other parents. There were times when Dr. McCandless *herself* would respond back to *my* e-mail, as well as other parents who were thirsting for information, and she would valiantly help to find answers to their difficult questions. God bless her for giving of her time and talent to help heal our children.

I must admit, as well, that it has taken me by far the longest to get around to writing this chapter than any other in the book. I think it is because there is just *so much* information on this subject, and I have had a hard time knowing where to start. That is exactly how I felt when we first learned our son had autism and when we first started to research all of the ways to treat his autism. It can be so overwhelming, and it is human instinct to want results *now!* But being so overburdened and having such a taxing child can be downright exhausting, so oftentimes parents procrastinate and do nothing, mostly because they have no idea how to begin. I am here to tell you that what you are feeling is more than okay, it is completely understandable, and before you do anything else, allow yourself to *breathe.* Be gentle with yourself, and calm your soul. Know that it is important to pace yourself. In the words of our Son-Rise teachers, always remember, "This is a *marathon,* not a *race!*"

One thing that encouraged me to pick up that pencil and get going with this chapter was hearing a light-hearted account from Dr. Henry Cloud. I do hope his experience will encourage you to "pick up your own pencil" and begin figuring out a plan. Dr. Cloud is a clinical psychologist, a co-host of a nationally-syndicated radio program, *New Life Live,* and the author of several books, including the million-seller *Boundaries,* which I mentioned briefly in chapter 3. He was speaking at a conference I attended a while back, and the conference was actually about how God has a dream for your life, and I wondered then if one of mine was to write this book! Well, Dr. Cloud had told a story about how when he was in graduate school, he had to complete his dissertation in a specific amount of time, and he had kept procrastinating, because he just didn't know where to begin. Well, one day, God spoke to him in a verse that came to him, Proverbs 6:6, "Go observe the ant, you sluggard, consider its ways and be wise!" Dr. Cloud thought that being referred to as a "sluggard" because he had procrastinated on his project may have been a bit harsh, but laughingly and admittedly, he was able to get to work on finishing his dissertation. The verse refers to the ant that carries just one grain of sand at a time but eventually ends up building a whole city! We, too, must be like the ant—me with writing this chapter, and perhaps you, as you take on the whole biomedical aspect of helping to heal and recover your child's health. It *is* a huge task, it *is* confusing, overwhelming, and exhausting ... but it is *not* impossible.

One grain of sand at a time … one idea, one concept, one new food to try, one new supplement to introduce … all will bring the final result of healing our child.

Exhausting? *Yes!* But Worth It

People have told me that what I've done with my son sounds so "exhausting" and like "so much work." Well, my answer to them has always been, "Yes! It was!" However, it was *exhausting* just *getting through the day*, before this, without any real improvement. *I'd much rather be intentionally exhausted for the purpose of guiding my child down the road to recovery than be unintentionally exhausted with nothing to show for it at the end of the day.* Yes, it is going to be hard work to treat your child biomedically, you bet. I will not lie to you and tell you it will be easy. *But* is it worth it to heal your child? Is it worth it to head toward recovery, whatever that means in each of our situations? Is it worth it to know that you've done everything you possibly could have done to help in any way imaginable, leaving no stone unturned? It would have been worth it even if I had never seen any improvement whatsoever, because at least I would have died knowing that I did my very best with the child God blessed me with. No regrets.

One Step at a Time

So, as we venture forward, just remember not to overwhelm yourself with feeling like you have to go out and do everything in every book having to do with biomedical treatment all at once, or even *ever* for that matter. There is a menu of options for you to choose from in this arena. You know your child best. You know what feels right and what doesn't. Some things that work for one child might not work for the next, and vice versa. Does this mean we don't try at all? No, of course not! It means we keep trying, one option at a time, one baby step at a time, one small grain of sand at a time, until we find what works for our child.

Do *not* do too many things at once, and remember—what did we just learn a few paragraphs before? This is a marathon, *not* a race. If you do too much at once, you will not know what is working and what isn't and what might work if we stopped doing something else. Aside from mixed results, you will mentally exhaust yourself to the point of giving up, and we never, ever want that to happen. So, take it slowly, do one or two things at a time, trial and error, fall off the horse, get back on, and all that good stuff. You may or may not choose to do each of the steps we will discuss later in this chapter, and that's okay. All of our kids are on a "spectrum," so you may or may not *have* to do all of these things with your child. You will know when you get there. You are not alone, and at this very moment, there are many other parents doing the exact same thing you are doing. Just keep plugging away until your "ant city" is built! I know it's scary, but charge ahead with confidence, just as it says in Proverbs 3:25–26, "Be not afraid of sudden fear ... for the Lord shall be thy confidence, and shall keep thy foot from being taken." Take that leap of faith, and you will not be disappointed, I assure you. On your marks! Get set! Go!

Our Road Leading to Biomedical Intervention

Okay, I hope you'll allow me to backtrack for a moment. I know we are all eager to forge ahead, but I'd like to walk with you down the road we took so that perhaps you may see some similarities in your own situation and perhaps may feel enlightened or at the very least encouraged as we let go of hands and part ways and you continue on without me.

I'd like to bring you back for a moment, to the point when we were still working with the original "team" from our local school district. Remember? The ones I was originally ready to send out of my house the day they came and first uttered the word autism to me, be it ever so gentle? Well, they had sent someone out not long after that day of giving me their "educated guess" that Aaren might have autism. At this point, we had not yet begun to explore the world of biomedical treatments for Aaren. He was on no special diets, was taking no supplements of any kind, and he was severely constipated. He was a self-selected finicky eater, eating mainly crackers, milk, macaroni and cheese, and bread. I would try to give him peaches and pears, which sometimes got eaten, and other times got thrown onto the floor. Other than that, he didn't eat anything but those foods, basically.

The team had sent out an early childhood special education teacher who came to our house once or twice a week to see Aaren. She would try to play with him and brought along a bag full of fun and interesting toys. However, the second she would step foot into our home, he would start to cry and scream. And God forbid if she would look at him or try to talk to him. The visits became very exhausting for both him and me. He would insist on my holding him while she was there and just could not tolerate her being in his personal space, looking at him, or trying to get him to interact. She stopped coming.

After that, an occupational therapist came to try to work with Aaren. He would sit and watch *Barney* (we decided to let him have the TV on, since he would not cry and scream, at least), but the second she would try to get his attention or interact with him, he would run and cry. One time he even hit her because she got too close. Hmmm … not working. We then had another specialist come out to work with him, a different special ed teacher who was wonderful at what she did, but unfortunately, again, it didn't make a difference in the case of Aaren. He would scream, cry, and throw himself on the floor the minute she would walk in. One time, he completely fell asleep during our visit—just conked out right on the floor from over-exhaustion, right in the middle of our conversation! The whole experience of having her there had just been too overwhelming and over-stimulating for him, and his whole body had just shut down. With heavy hearts, the teachers said there just wasn't anymore that they could do at this point, as far as home visits. They suggested medication, at least for his apparent anxiety—perhaps this would calm him down enough so that they could attempt to work with him again. So, we made another appointment with a doctor, this time a developmental pediatrician.

Medication Trial

Aaren was put on Zoloft for a short period of time. At first we thought it might be helping, but soon it was apparent that it just wasn't solving much of anything, and in fact, it might be making matters worse. Plus, with Aaren's severe constipation issues, we had enough trouble trying to give him medications and/or over-the-counter treatments for *that*. Forcing an awful-tasting Zoloft liquid into his body every day on top of everything else was just too much for him and us, so we decided to take him off of the Zoloft. Our pediatrician said that we could safely give Aaren an enema every other day for the constipation, since all of the things we had tried to use for that had not been working very well, either. So ... we thought we would lessen the burden of giving medications, which helped some, but giving the enemas every other day was no picnic either. I kept wondering, "Where *are* you, God? I surrendered, I'm waiting for your guidance, and yet you sit there and do *nothing*!" That is surely how it felt, but I knew in my heart that he never leaves us nor forsakes us. I had to hang onto that. I had to believe there was hope in a world that seemed completely hopeless. Some days I could manage to do that, but other days it seemed that defeat was inevitable. Things were falling apart, *not* coming together as I thought they should now that we had a diagnosis. This was not getting any easier. Relief was not ours. I was frustrated and found myself having to surrender again and again, sometimes many times in one day!

My Quest for Answers—the DAN! Protocol

I began looking at the concept of diet, to try to help Aaren with his extreme constipation, knowing that his diet wasn't helping him, but that we also couldn't continue to give him enemas on a regular basis. This was not how God intended things to be. Our bodies should not have to rely on enemas, especially at two years of age. Somehow, somewhere along the way, his body had malfunctioned or become overburdened. It was crying out to be healed, its cry showing itself in excruciating ways. The time had come to an end, and I was bound and determined to find some answers and get things changed for Aaren. I couldn't stand to watch him suffer anymore.

I began to devour everything I could get my hands on about constipation in children and surprisingly found that entangled in all of my research were several accounts of children with autism suffering from severe constipation. Others suffered from just the opposite, chronic diarrhea, but both were quite common in this subset of children. I didn't realize that the constipation and the autism had anything to do with one another, but it soon became apparent that they certainly can.

In my quest for knowledge about healing my son's constipation, I inadvertently stumbled upon something called the "DAN! Protocol," (DAN! stands for Defeat Autism Now!), which is a series of treatments used in the process of biomedical intervention for the treatment of autism. "DAN! Doctors are trained in the 'DAN! Protocol,' an approach to autism treatment which starts with the idea that autism is a biomedical disorder, specifically. DAN! Doctors feel that autism is a disorder caused by a combination of lowered immune response, external toxins from vaccines and other sources, and problems caused by certain foods" (Rudy 2007). DAN! Doctors treat the disorder based on those beliefs.

This movement was started by Bernard Rimland, PhD, who was also the founder and director of the Autism Research Institute in San Diego, California, back in the 60s. He also founded the Autism Society of America and was an internationally recognized authority on autism spectrum disorders. He was also the father of a high-functioning autistic son, so I believe his heart was in his work, and it showed. Rimland passed away in 2006, but his legacy lives on, and I know my son wouldn't be where he is today without the work and dedication of Rimland.

DAN! doctors can be a great resource to you as you proceed with the steps below, and I would recommend touching base with a DAN! doctor even if you, like I did, do some or most of the interventions listed by yourself. Some of your choices will include the need for a certified doctor, and I would recommend a DAN! doctor. I was able to find a certified DAN! doctor in my area whose services were covered by insurance, although many are not. Be sure to ask when you are setting up an appointment. To find a DAN! doctor in your area, you can log onto the Autism Research Institute at www.autism.com for both domestic and international doctors. Parents are welcomed and encouraged to attend DAN! conferences, which are generally held twice a year. Learn more at www.danconference.com.

Leaky Gut Syndrome

The first part of the treatment protocol includes implementing a special diet, called the gluten-free/casein-free, or GF/CF diet, which is a diet that excludes the use of gluten (found in grains such as wheat, oats, barley, and rye) and casein (found in all dairy products or other products containing dairy). The reason for the diet, I learned, is that scientific researchers had been finding that the casein and gluten, which are actually proteins specifically called caseo*morphine*, and gluteo*morphin*, were not being broken down properly in the bodies of children with autism. In children with autism, these particles were found "floating around in the bloodstream" and could be detected in urine. Once these substances were then transported to the brain, they seemed to have an "opioid-like effect," according to McCandless, "with a potency several times that of morphine." Morphine is a naturally occurring phenanthrene alkaloid of opium, and a very powerful drug used as a painkiller. Scientists named the unusual particles found in these children's bodies "opioids."

This condition, that is, being unable to break down proteins crucial to proper digestion and nutritional absorption, I learned, was referred to as the "leaky gut syndrome." Children suffering from a "leaky gut" may appear to be "spacey" or "in their own world" and often don't feel pain in ways that other children do, just as someone under the influence of morphine does not feel pain as they would without its use. Leaky gut syndrome can also cause constipation, or just the opposite, diarrhea. In essence, as I understood it, it was as if I was virtually "poisoning" my son every time I fed him a food that contained gluten or casein. Without realizing it, I was feeding him the foods that only exacerbated the problem.

Dr. McCandless confirms the notion of a leaky gut and its need for healing, stating, "Scientific studies are pointing to inflammation in the gut being caused by gluten, casein, soy and other foods." She goes on to say that this is not seen as an allergy, but rather, something that is called, "T-cell inflammatory response to these foods." Furthermore, she states, "In a study conducted by Dr. H. Jyonouchi from the University of Minnesota, it was shown that 75 percent of the children with autism spectrum disorder have T-cell reactivity to foods." The GF/CF diet is one of the "single most effective actions you can take on your own to begin to help your child," according to McCandless.

In my quest to find out how Aaren may have gotten leaky gut syndrome, I found that there were varying differences as to why or how a child might be prone to the condition. Scientists had different ideas as to why this phenomenon occurred in these children, from what I could tell. One theory, given by a researcher named Andrew Wakefield, seemed to be very convincing to me. He had some pretty striking evidence, in my opinion, surmising that the culprit could lead back to childhood vaccinations, just as I had feared. In 1998, Wakefield and some of his colleagues published a study in the prestigious English medical journal *Lancet* that claimed to show a connection between the MMR vaccine and autism. Wakefield's theory was that the MMR vaccine, which contains a live virus, can cause in susceptible children a chronic measles infection. This in turn leads to gastrointestinal disturbances, including what he calls a leaky gut syndrome, which then allows for certain toxins and chemicals, like those from bread and dairy that are normally broken down by the gut, to enter the bloodstream, where they can access and damage the developing brain (Novella 200). What this was telling me, as I understood it, was that when the immune system is compromised, as when receiving a vaccination, especially one including thimerisol (remember, in chapter 2 we learned that thimerisol is a mercury derivative), the body's natural function of detoxification is impaired, and susceptibility to a leaky gut is increased.

I went on to read that some children with autism had a family history of digestion problems as well as celiac disease. My mother-in-law was properly diagnosed with this disorder at the age of seventy-two, not long after we found out Aaren had autism. Celiac disease is a disease in which "the lining of the small intestine is damaged due to ingestion of gluten and similar proteins, which are found in wheat, oats, barley, and other grains including hybrid grains such as triticale," and " its development requires a genetically predisposed person who is eating those foods," (Lewis 2006). However, from what I read, even if those factors are present, a person may not develop celiac disease until a "trigger factor" (like childhood vaccinations, for instance) starts the abnormal immune system response. Again, had I known this information earlier, I would definitely have re-calculated the giving of immunizations for my son.

All of this information validated even more for me that I would need to begin a GF/CF diet for Aaren, but I knew it would be a huge undertaking. For help on getting started on the GF/CF diet and how to implement it, you can go to www.gfcfdiet.com, and click on the link on the very bottom of the screen that says, "Beginning the Diet." I also found great benefit from purchasing two books by Lisa Lewis, entitled, *Special Diets for Special Kids* and *Special Diets for Special Kids II*. Her books offer a variety of recipes and helpful information on sustaining a GF/CF diet. Another helpful line of books are those written by Betty Hagman, but keep in mind her recipes are *gluten free* only, and not necessarily casein free. You will have to modify some of her recipes to make it work for the GF/CF diet, but her knowledge of gluten-free flours is well worth the time to peruse her books. I would substitute rice milk or almond milk if a recipe called for milk, and a dairy-free/casein-free version of non-allowed items like butter, sour cream, and cream cheese. There are several casein-free versions of these products out in the market today.

At this point, you may want to consider allergy testing for your child, but it is a personal choice. I have used "muscle testing" as a form of allergy testing for foods, and also to determine certain supplement compatibility for Aaren and for others in our family through the use of a neuro-chiropractic specialist. I did not do this when Aaren was younger. However, it is something I did later, to help us with "nutrition maintenance."

Immunity Up, Toxic Load Down

Along with beginning Aaren on the diet, I also gathered that I would need to find a way to build his immunity up. One way to do that, I read, was to bring his toxic load *down*. The Generation Rescue Web site was a wonderful resource for me in this area and others, and I strongly urge you to check it out at www. www.generationrescue.org. At the time I was using the site, Jenny McCarthy was not involved with the organization, but it is now one that she endorses. On the site, you will find information on her and her son, as well as other stories of recovery. You will also find a vast array of information on the aspect of biomedical interventions and the treatments that are available. I found that there was a lot of information offered, and I chose to pick and choose which treatments felt right for us. I encourage you to do the same.

1.   Low or No Sugar

To bring Aaren's toxic load down, I first decided to do the GF/CF diet, as discussed earlier, I slowly started baking with fructose instead of sugar and later found I had excellent results with brown rice syrup in all of my baked goods. I made sure Aaren's diet was low in sugar or that I didn't use sugar at all in the first place, but I also didn't overdo it on the fructose or the brown rice syrup. Also, I chose not to give Aaren soy of any kind, as research shows that oftentimes children on the spectrum will have just as much trouble breaking down the soy protein as they do the casein and the gluten protein. I stayed away from it altogether to avoid possible problems.

It is at this point, as well, that you could choose to have allergy testing done for your child. According to the Generation Rescue Web site, "an ELISA blood test measuring IgE and IgG anti-bodies will help you determine your child's food sensitivities." We opted to forego testing, but if you do choose to do so, please talk to your DAN! doctor about ordering the tests.

2.   Go Organic!

Next, I decided to take that one step further and "go organic!" Since it is expensive to do so, the rest of the family did not partake. If you can afford to do it, I do believe everyone could benefit from going organic. For Aaren, though, I bought only organic and chemical-free food, shampoo, soap, laundry detergent, and fluoride-free toothpaste. You can find organic and chemical-free goods at a health store, on-line, and often at your local grocery store. When choosing to go organic, you must also be wary of things such as nitrates in meats and aspartame used as a sweetener. These both add stress to the body and are not natural.

3. Nutritional Supplements

Because Aaren's nutrition was compromised, due to his diet and his inflamed gut, I began to supplement his diet with nutrients. This is where I found myself going page by page through *Children with Starving Brains*, reading over and over what Dr. McCandless suggested. Her first order up was to find a basic multi-vitamin and mineral, excluding copper, and she listed other must-have nutrients we could start giving him right away. I was *on it!* The multi-vitamin we used was in liquid form (easier to absorb, gentle on the system) and was one that I ordered from Brain Child Nutritionals. You can find their Web site at www.brainchildnutritionals.com. For more specific supplements we added later on, I also used a liquid form from a company called E-lyte Liquid Minerals. You can find their products as well as several other products at www.autismcoach.com.

4. Fish Oil

To maintain Aaren's brain health, I began using cod liver oil and fish oil. The cod liver oil was used so that Aaren could obtain proper doses of vitamin A, since, according to McCandless, "infants and many children are not able to convert non-toxic beta-carotene to Vitamin A, so though important for itself carotenes cannot be relied upon as a source of Vitamin A." Basically, this meant to me that he was not getting a sufficient supply of vitamin A from his multi-vitamin alone, because he most likely was not breaking down the beta carotene sufficiently. We used Nordic Naturals Arctic Cod Liver Oil, which you can find at www.omega-direct.com. I supplemented his diet with fish oil to help with his brain development and maintenance. McCandless states that the Omega-3 fatty acids "help improve the immune response," and also "work against inflammation in the GI tract," as well as maintain "neurotransmitter, cellular, and membrane integrity." You can find fish oil at the omega-direct Web site, as well. Feel free to shop around for pricing and quality, but we found Nordic Naturals to be one of the better quality products out there.

5. Digestive Enzymes

To help Aaren's digestion, I got the book *Enzymes for Autism and other Neurological Conditions*, by Karen DeFelice and started to use digestive enzymes. I learned how to make "enzyme balls" and was sure to give him those with each meal. I went to Karen's Web site at www.enzymestuff.com and found several ideas on how to get him to take the enzymes, and we found that putting them in a "peanut butter ball" worked wonderfully for us. I would also put some calcium powder in his enzyme ball at the same time, so that he would have that extra boost of calcium at each meal, since he no longer drank milk, and I could not get him to drink rice milk, almond milk, coconut milk, or any other milk allowed on the GF/CF diet. The Web site has so many other practical ideas, it is well worth a visit. DeFelice is also a very present source on the site and has answered my questions directly via e-mail in the past. The line of enzymes we chose to use for Aaren were Houston Enzymes, ordered from their Web site located at www.houston-enzymes.com. I was extremely pleased with their fast service, and Dr. Houston himself or his staff answered my questions quickly and efficiently. They were nothing but supportive.

On a quick side note, I would encourage you to see DeFelice's book and learn more about viruses in the body if you feel this might affect your child. If a virus lingers, it could "lead to some gastrointestinal and/or neurological problems," according to DeFelice. Protease enzymes are "an excellent therapy to use against a virus," she states. You will find more information in her book or on her Web site regarding the specifics on those enzymes and/or their use. At this point, you may also choose to consult your DAN! doctor regarding this issues, and the two of you can decide if prescribing an antifungal medication like Valtrex or Famvir. According to McCandless, "rotating anti-virals sometimes seems to help maintain responsiveness to the drugs," and she strongly advises "'safety' tests for blood count and chemistries" since these types of medications may stress the liver. We did not have to do this with Aaren, but it is a worthy point to bring up, and I wanted you to be aware of this aspect of treatment as well.

How Will They Take Their Supplements?

You might ask *how* on earth we got our son to take all of these supplements. That's a very good question! He could not swallow pills at the time, and so I would make sure to buy supplements either in capsule form or in liquid form. I would then put the content from the capsule or the liquid supplement into his drink, which was usually watered-down juice, and sure enough, he would drink his cocktail of supplements for me. I always made sure to give him something I knew he liked to eat along with his drink, and preferably something that would make him thirsty. With many of the supplements, it is best to give a dose two or three times per day, so I would either give it with a snack or with a meal.

When we started on enzymes, I found that he would eat those for me if I put them into a "peanut butter ball." I found that idea on the "enzymestuff" Web site, and it worked like a charm for us. I could make up a big batch of his "enzyme balls" and keep them in the freezer, and then each time he was ready to eat, we would take one out and he would eat that first. It became such a habit for him, that in time, if I would somehow forget or give him his food first, he would quickly remind me and say, "Mommy, don't forget my enzyme ball!"

So, making an "enzyme ball" or a "nutrient ball" might work for you, or whipping up a "cocktail" might do the trick for your child— or, you might find something else altogether that works better. The key is to start slow. Keep in mind, I'm giving you a ton of information here, and much of what we did happened slowly over time. We didn't add everything all at once, so he had time to get used to new textures or tastes. It seems daunting at first, but it truly will become second nature once you get into the swing of things.

Another tidbit of information I will share with you that worked well with us is to write down everything that you are giving your child and when and exactly *how*, and tape it on a piece of paper to the inside of a cupboard in the kitchen. This way, if you need to be gone for some reason and it is time for your child to have his or her "drink" or "enzyme ball," etc., this will ensure that he or she will get exactly what he or she needs, whether it is from Grandma, Mom, Dad, or a friend who is watching your child at the time. Hang in there; you will find your groove.

6.   Epsom Salt Baths

Still trying to get the toxic load down and the immunity up, I decided to start giving Aaren baths with Epsom salts. According to DeFelice (2005), a doctor named Dr. Rosemary Waring found that, "most children on the autism spectrum are very low in sulfate and may be as low as 15 percent of the amount in neurologically typical people." Epsom salt acts as a natural detoxifier and also supplies magnesium sulfate to the child taking the bath. The mineral is absorbed into the body through the skin. For more information on Epsom salt baths and other ways of using Epsom salt as a detoxification mechanism, go to www.enzymestuff.com/epsomsalts.htm. Interestingly, I learned that a lack of magnesium can contribute to restless leg syndrome, which I am sure my son suffered from. His legs would thrash around while he slept, and he rarely got a good night's sleep because of it (me either, for that matter!). He no longer has those symptoms.

7.   Probiotics—Anti-Fungal Medications

Probiotic supplements are used to replenish the amount of "good bacteria" we have in our intestine at any given time. You may have heard of people taking probiotics such as acidophilus, which is found in yogurt, after they had completed taking a round of antibiotics. This would make sense, because the use of antibiotics causes both our good *and* bad bacteria to be destroyed, so adding acidophilus—a "good" bacteria—after completing a round of antibiotics would replenish our good bacteria and hopefully restore our desired healthy intestinal flora. However, when antibiotics are used often, as in treating ear infections or other types of infections, our number of *good* bacteria diminishes right along with the *bad* bacteria. In the absence of the *good* bacteria, or when our immune system is compromised in some way, our bodies can be more prone to invasions of yeast or other bacterial fungus.

According to McCandless (2002), "Children with impaired immune systems and inflamed intestines are particularly vulnerable to invastions by fungi, especially yeast of the Candida species." Not only can the absence of good bacteria severely impair digestion and assimilation of nutrients, but it can also cause a host of other problems, especially for children on the autism spectrum. It can cause an overgrowth of yeast, the most popular type called "Candida," which we discussed in chapter 4, and it can also cause an overgrowth of other bacteria such as clostridia. As we touched on earlier, side effects of an overgrowth of yeast and bacteria can be but are not limited to: hyperactivity, giggling at inappropriate times or a "hyper giggle," short attention span, visual stims or other self-stimulatory behaviors, "spaciness," irritability, anger, aggression (including head banging, which my son was the *king* of!), sound sensitivity, vestibular sensory issues, poor eye contact, tantrums, hand flapping, and more.

You can talk with your DAN! doctor about possibly prescribing an anti-fungal medication for your child, such as Nystatin, Diflucan, Bactrim, or Vancomycin. You can look into testing possibilities on your own at the Great Plains Laboratory at www.greatplainslaboratory. com or at the Great Smokies Diagnostic Laboratory at www. genovadiagnostics.com. There are some "natural" and over the counter treatment methods you can choose from to treat yeast and bacteria, such as treating with a probiotic (we chose Ther-Biotics Complete from Klaire Laboratories). Or you can use products like Colloidal Silver, Olive Leaf Extract, or oil of oregano to treat bacteria, and products such as biotin, garlic, caprylic acid, grape seed oil, or an enzyme called "No-phenol" (which you will find at the enzyme stuff Web site listed earlier in this chapter) to treat yeast. You may also be interested in putting your child on a yeast-free diet, such as the SCD (Specific Carbohydrate Diet) that we briefly discussed in chapter 4. Log onto http://www.pecanbread.com for more detailed information on the diet, specifically. For more information on this topic and much, much more, from a mother's point of view (whose experience has taught her so much and brought her children so far …) see http://www.danasview.net/yeast.htm.

There are many more options, as well, so this is a time to see what works best and feels right for your family. Do some research, talk with your DAN! doctor, do what works for your child. When working with natural or homeopathic products, much of what you encounter will be trial and error. Every child is so different, what works for some might not work for others. Just keep trying until you find what works for yours. We did use probiotics, as I stated earlier, but we also asked our doctor to prescribe a round of Diflucan for our son. He was on this medication for an entire month, and I do think it helped a lot. However, word to the wise … in doing many of these treatments, do not be flustered if things get worse before they get better. It is bound to happen! Oftentimes you will see a "die-off" effect when treating for yeast or bacteria, and also when the body is detoxing in general. As it gets rid of its "waste," it causes the body to react, and some of that is normal. You your doctor will need to judge if you feel you should cut back on a dosage or try a new treatment route, etc. We do not want this experience to be miserable for you *or* your child, and remember, this is a *marathon*, not a race. We don't have to try to fix everything in one day. Don't be in a rush to do too much too fast, or you may really see some negative reactions in your child, and that will be hard on you, but it will also be hard on them. Think it through, and proceed with a confident caution.

8.   **Chelation**

Yes, I think we've finally come to the end! You'll notice that chelation (pronounced 'kee-LAY-shun') is at the end of our list, and it's for good reason I put it there. It is *vital* that you save this for your last step. Chelation is the process of detoxification, in this instance, in relation to heavy metal detoxification. If this is done too early in the healing process, the DAN! Chelation protocol document states that, "Attempting heavy metal detoxification before the patient's underlying gastrointestinal and nutritional problems are corrected will likely be disappointing." Not only that, it can cause further problems and complicate matters even more. If the gut isn't healed, it doesn't pay to waste your time with chelation, and in fact, you will do more harm than good for your child. If the body isn't strong in nutrients and minerals, it will not be able to withstand the pressure of chelating. The immune system cannot be compromised when beginning chelation—on the contrary! We want to achieve optimum health first and then begin to excrete metals in the last "cleansing phase" of healing the body.

As we discussed earlier in chapter 4 in regard to thimerisol usage in vaccines (as well as other injectables) being a point of toxicity for our kids on the spectrum, so too can other environmental toxins be adding to their heavy metal load. Many of us are exposed to heavy metal toxicity every day, whether we know it or not. Heavy metals are found in the earth's crust, a part of our very soil. The air we breathe and the food we eat contain minute quantities of toxic metals, but these quantities add up, especially if our immune system is down, and our body is unable to excrete the toxins as it should. Foods like fish, particularly tuna and swordfish, are highly susceptible. If we cook our fish using an aluminum pan, we've just added to our toxic intake. If we use anti-perspirant containing aluminum, we are exposed to heavy metals, and if you have those silver fillings, (called amalgam fillings) in your mouth from when you were a kid? Yup, you are definitely exposed to heavy metals. Dr. Boyd Haley, the chair and professor of the chemistry department at the University of Kentucky, responded to an article titled, "Mercury Dental Fillings Do Not Pose Health Risk," in quite a determined manner when he said, "This article, and the supporting comments by panel members and dentists, represents an intellectual travesty and an ethical failure of the government and dental agencies whose assignment is to protect Americans, especially American children, from exposure to neurotoxins" (Davis 2004). Please think twice before filling your child's mouth with amalgam fillings! And yours, for that matter!

Our kids, too, have been exposed to heavy metals, but in their case, a build-up has collected, their immune system has drastically lowered, and it is impairing their body's ability to detoxify as necessary to become healthy. So, we look to chelation, *once the gut is healed* and the *child's immune system is strong.*

Chelation Testing

In the area of chelation, you have many options. Some of your options will require a physician's assistance, while other "natural" choices may be done by parents. If you do decide to use a natural chelator, as we did, I would strongly suggest you at the very least check ind with your DAN! doctor or physician before, during, and after the process is completed. You can talk with your doctor about preliminary testing that should be done, perhaps using tests such as a CBC (complete blood count) with differential platelets, the comprehensive metabolic panel, and the thyroid panel (T3, T4, TSH), which all include a blood draw (McCandless 2002). McCandless also recommends a urinalysis, a hair elements test, the OAT test (Organic Acid Test), and a comprehensive/digestive stool anaylsis. Again, these are all things for you to talk over with your doctor. In our case, Aaren had such strong anxiety that when we did try to do a blood draw on him at a routine doctor's visit when he was fifteen to eighteen months old, it took three nurses, myself, and finally a *tourniquet* to strap him down, and even then, they ended up taking blood from his foot. *Never again,* I swore to myself, unless absolutely necessary.

I knew that in our case, we would need to go with the most non-invasive type of testing we could, and so I chose to do the urinalysis and the hair elements test. The urinalysis was done through my doctor's office, and I did the hair elements test on my own, right from home. To find out more about doing the elements test yourself, and how to read the results (you may also want to follow up with your DAN! doctor and bring in the results from these tests to him or her, as we did), go to: http://home.earthlink.net/~moriam/HOW_TO_hair_test.html or just type in "hair elements test" to bring you to this link. As you continue on the chelation path, you will want to do more testing to see the results of the chelation process. We definitely saw improvements in behaviors and more alert, higher level thinking (this is when we first noticed Aaren starting to be silly—on purpose, and very appropriately. We didn't *know* he had a sense of humor!)

Our Chelator of Choice

In the chelating agent arena, again, you are offered several choices. I chose to go with a natural, over-the-counter chelating agent that was recommended in *Children with Starving Brains,* called Authia cream, by Westlake Laboratories, Inc. You can purchase this product at various sites online. We chose to order through a company located at www.spectrumsupplements.com. Authia cream is a transdermal alithiamine, or "TTFD" for short, which provides highly absorbable forms of bitamin B1 (TTFD) and bitamin B12 (Methyl Cobalamin). According to McCandless (2002), research performed by Derrick Lonsdale, MD, has shown that the use of TTFD has been found to be beneficial in treating "8 of 10 ASD children." The thing that appealed to me was that Authia cream is a transdermal cream, which means it is applied topically ... on top of the skin. This makes the application process very easy and manageable. This seemed right for us, and sounded much easier than using an oral form of chelation, or an agent in the form of a shot. I looked into many different types of chelators, and this one, by far, looked the best *for us*.

We applied the Authia cream on Aaren's back each day, so that he would not touch it (see *Children with Starving Brains* for dosage information). It did not sting or itch or anything like that, so he never fought it, and in fact, he liked having me massage his back with the lotion. It did not take us long (less than a week) to notice that Aaren started emitting an odor that smelled like metal! We were not the only ones who noticed it, either! His speech therapist was one of the first persons to say, "What's that awful smell?" Aaren also began to sweat through his head when he would sleep, either during the day or at night. This, too, was a good sign that detoxification was happening, because toxins can come out through our skin, most often in the form of a rash or some sort, or through sweat.

On a funny side note, there was a mom I had been talking to around this time who also had a son with autism. Her son was twenty-two years old at the time, and she was trying some of the things I had recommended that she hadn't already tried herself (don't get me wrong, she is another "warrior mom," as Jenny McCarthy would say—she moved heaven and earth to help her son thus far and was still not ready to give up on him). Well, she bought some Authia cream used it with her son, and shortly afterwards reported to me that her son started to emit a terrible odor that could be smelled throughout the house! I explained the detoxification process, and we both had to laugh. She has seen some wonderful gains in her son's progress since then. Not long after that, he had said to her through his communication device (he is nonverbal), "Mom, I'm not stupid. everyone thinks I am, but I'm not. I want to go to college." He did take some art classes, and she said he was so talented—she never knew. Was it worth the smell? You bet!

Other Chelating Agents

There are other types of chelators, as I said, and I will not name them all here, but some types of natural or over-the-counter chelators you can look into are: NDF Plus, PCA-Rx, RNA drops, EDTA, clay baths, cilantro, ALA, and selenium to list a few. Prescription chelating agents include DMSA, DMPS, and EDTA.

Keep it Simple—Get Organized!

As we wrap up this chapter, please keep in mind, there is a lot of information for you to digest, process, and research, based on what you've read. With your head spinning, and information making you feel like you are swirling and twirling around headed for the big black hole of the universe, it might seem impossible to keep this simple, right? I know exactly what you are saying, but do keep in mind, this won't last forever, and you won't need to do it all *today!* Start slowly, and work up. Remember, I have sat right where you are sitting today. I have been in your shoes. I feel your pain, and I sympathize, When it seems like you can't, just remember, *you can*, and more importantly, *you must*. Your child is depending on you—you can do it! Pray about it, ask God to give you strength and wisdom every step of the way, and realize you do not walk alone. Just as Philippians 4:13 says, "I can do all things through Christ which strengthens me," know that this is one of those times.

At this point, I would strongly suggest you go back and start again at number, read through each step, and begin to highlight what jumps out at you, what *feels right*. It will be different for every one of you, as each of our children are at different places on the spectrum, and each child is so individually different. Take what pertains to your child and leave the rest. Don't let it scare or overwhelm you. You can always come back again later to see if you've missed anything. Next, start jotting down a rough sketch, or framework, of the plan you would like to create for your child's biomedical intervention. Get it down on paper and out of your head, and you won't feel quite so overwhelmed. Plus, you will have something concrete to look at or to bring with you to the doctor.

Begin to scour the Internet for other sites that could help you to understand even more about all of the things you have written down in your plan, and connect yourself to several different listservs and discussion forums to connect with other parents and professionals. It is so nice to be able to bounce ideas off of others who understand exactly what you are going through or what situation you are working through *today*. We, as parents of these fascinating children, can provide a *wealth of information* to one another, simply because we've been to the *school of hard knocks* and we've learned a thing or two!

Be sure to go to your local library and check out the books I've suggested or any others that you feel you would like to look into. You will get a feel for the books you decide are a "must have," and you can buy those specific ones to refer to, make notes in, etc. Be sure to jot down any notes or pertinent information that you've learned from the books you decide not to buy, because then you will still have the information at your fingertips. I would suggest organizing your notes before they are all a jumbled mess and they all start to look like one big blur! If it helps you, use color-coded folders for each different subject, such as "GF/CF diet," or "chelation." Then, as you get more tidbits of information you feel would be beneficial in those certain areas, you can make a copy or jot down an idea on paper and throw it into the appropriate folder. You can certainly do this on your computer, as well, and create separate documents with information relating to a specific topic, if you'd like. Whatever works for you is just fine. The point is, find a system, and *use it!* This will help you to stay the course when the road gets bumpy, to find your way if your map gets tossed out the window.

Chapter 6

Bringing It All Together in Faith, Hope, and Love

*"If you CAN?" said Jesus. "Everything is
possible for him who believes."*

— Mark 9:23 (Healing a boy of an evil spirit.)

I am so proud of you for getting this far. This proves that you are in the driver's seat, ready to go to the ends of the earth and back if you have to. I just want to take a moment to remind you that even if this is hard right now, it won't be hard forever! Have faith in what you do not see! Every case is different, of course, but in our situation with Aaren, we put in a strong and intense three years, and we will reap the rewards of that labor of love forever. I would do it all again in a heartbeat, every single bit of it. I would like to summarize a few areas of our journey for you and lay out some time lines for you that I think might be helpful. I hope it will get you excited for what lies ahead and that you are motivated by that excitement.

We used the Son-Rise therapy for a solid one and a half years, and then were able to end our program. Does this mean you will be able to stop your program in a year and a half? No, not necessarily. Remember, each child is different, and each family is different as well. Don't worry about how long it will take you. Just invest in your child each day, and let the time take care of itself. Did we stop using Son-Rise philosophies in our child-rearing practices? No, we didn't. It has been weaved into the tapestry of our parenting style, added to the toolbox of our parenting tools, and it has become a way of life in many respects. However, we no longer have the need for a formal playroom stocked with rotating volunteers who work with our son one-on-one. But is some one-on-one time still good for our son? Of course! And it is just as important that we spend that time with our other two sons or with each other as husband and wife. Again, we've kept some of the principles of the program, but we no longer need to keep the program itself.

In the area of diet and nutrition, it certainly seemed like a daunting task laid out before us to take on the GF/CF diet, but you know what? We only did the diet, and I mean *did* the diet 100 percent (I believe it's got to be *all or nothing*, at least at first), for about nine months. Yes, you heard correctly, only nine months! At around the nine-month mark, I began to read about the use of digestive enzymes and how there was a specific enzyme used for children with autism who have trouble breaking down gluten and casein. According to what I read, some families were having wonderful results using *enzymes alone* and not doing a GF/CF diet at all. It is something you can consider for your child, but we did not do things that way, so I do not have the experience to share. However, when we did begin the enzymes, I then started to challenge Aaren with foods that did contain gluten and casein, making sure he had enzymes with every single particle of food or drink that entered his system! Slowly, I would add one new food at a time and then watch him like a hawk, looking for physical signs such as red cheeks or a skin rash, possible constipation, or loose stools, and I would also be aware of any behavioral changes I might see—positive or negative. In this way, we proceeded for another year or so, and some wonderful things happened. I think his leaky gut healed itself, and he also started to branch out and eat a variety of foods. *This* from a child who only ate a handful of foods before we began ... now he was eating broccoli, carrots, ham, turkey, hamburger, pineapple, and so many more things like the best of them! From what I read, once their gut heals, they will start to crave the foods that their body needs for proper nutrition, and they will start to eat things you never dreamed they would! That is *exactly* how it happened for us! Now, does this mean you will be able to stop the diet in nine months, or that you will not have to do it at all because you can use digestive enzymes? Again, this is a personal choice and something you will need to consider for your child and your situation. Some families have chosen to remain gluten free/casein free for life. It is a personal choice that only you can make.

We still try to keep the toxic load down in Aaren the best that we can, but I will say I slipped away from buying everything organic for him, simply because I started to see he was not reacting to certain foods or shampoos, etc. And so, because of affordability issues as well, I slipped back into buying things that were not necessarily organic. Would it still be the best way to go if we could? Yes, you bet. I have no doubt. I do make an effort, though, and we have changed some of the things we all eat or use as a family. I still bake with brown rice syrup and organic flour, and Aaren still does not drink milk (neither do I). I still give Epsom salt baths now and then, and I do continue to supplement his diet with probiotics and certain nutrients. I try to incorporate some of what I learned and *had* to do for so long and tried to make some lasting changes based on the knowledge I've acquired from doing so.

As of this writing, Aaren is seven years old and is in the first grade. His teacher says he is a wonderful student. His report cards look great, and he is learning to read. He no longer carries the diagnosis of autism, and he also has been tested by a behavioral neurologist and does not meet criteria for Asperger's, PDD-Nos, or any other spectrum disorder. He does still have a language processing disorder that may cause a learning disability of some sort down the road, but so far so good, and we are doing everything we can to prevent that from happening.

He has play dates with friends and birthday party invites. He is in Cub Scouts and plans to play soccer in the spring. He does not receive speech therapy, OT, or any other type of therapy. He loves to play with our dog, Hunter, and with his big brothers. *Spongebob Squarepants* is a favorite, as well as iCarly and *SuperNanny*. He loves playing Connect Four, Yahtzee, and Sorry! He and I built a snowman together this winter, and when we came in to get some hot cocoa, he said, "Mommy, I loved building a snowman with you. That was the most fun I've ever had with you in my *whole life.*" *This* from a child who, four years ago, was completely nonverbal and would scream and bang his head 90 percent of the day. Moments like that make it all worthwhile. A tear forms in my eye at the mere thought of where we were and how far we've come.

Now, does all of this mean he is "perfect"? No, of course not, but is any child? We are still dealing with some possible "residual effects" of his autism, although at times I wonder where the autism left off and his natural temperament took over! He has a quick temper at times and hates losing at games. We are working on that. We talk about using our words and taking deep breaths. He gets shy, especially around people he doesn't know well or when he's in a large group, and we are working on that. We talk about giving a friendly smile, even if we aren't sure of what to say, and we come up with things we might talk about next time. He sometimes gets overwhelmed and plays loudly or becomes agitated. We are working on that. We talk about quiet voices in the house and about finding a quiet place to go to calm our bodies. We talk about squeezing a pillow or asking for a hug. As you will see, we are still in the race. The marathon is not completely over for us, perhaps, but that's okay. I'd like to think that we are taking our "victory lap," and I'd love to have you running beside me someday. Lace up those track shoes and come along. I'll be cheering for you every step of the way. Run on love, run on determination, run on hope alone if you have to, but just run. Never, *ever* let anyone take away your hope. In an article posted on the Autism Treatment Center of America website, found at www.autismtreatmentcenter. org, titled, "Autism and the Myth of False Hope," Raun Kaufman has said, "There is no such thing as *false hope!*" He goes on to say that "The very idea of "false hope" means that there are times when hoping can be bad, wrong, or inappropriate. Because I have seen over and over again, in my life and in the lives of countless others, that hoping only helps and never hurts, I do not believe that hope can ever be "false." I wholeheartedly agree. Hope is *yours*, no matter what the doctors say, no matter what your friends say, no matter what your mother-in-law or your next door neighbor says … hope is *yours*, and *no one* can take it from you.

Surrender, have faith, have hope, and love your child with all of your being no matter the circumstance, no matter the behavior, no matter what the *world* says you've got. *Proceed with purpose*, and listen closely to that still, small voice. Before you know it, you will have ideas you've never thought of before. You will be led to people you would never have dreamed of meeting or befriending, or to places you would not have thought to go to on your own. Circumstances will come together in an odd sort of way—but later you will see it wasn't so odd after all, it made perfect sense, and you will see that God had his hand on you the entire time. He was working in your life, even though you didn't think anything was working at all.

He *will* speak to you! Maybe not in a thunderous voice like we would imagine, maybe not with miracles and lightning bolts … but he's there, and he *will* show you the way if you will open yourself up to him. One of my favorite Christian songs is "Mighty to Save," by Laura Story (http://www.youtube.com/watch?v=-qNOMLS6weE), which talks about how God can move the mountains, and isn't this so true? There is *nothing* that God can't do. However, sometimes he might want *us* to move or grow in some way, and may intend *not* to move our "mountain," so that we can survive *through it* and come out stronger for doing so. As quoted by Beth Moore, from her Bible Study Series/DVD entitled, *Living Beyond Yourself,* (1998) oftentimes "we want God to change our circumstances, but He wants to change US!" Be open to hear from Him, and in the meantime, when you are "in limbo" believe with all of your heart that this *will* get better; no one will stop you but God, and if He stops you, He's got another direction He wants you to go in. Find peace and joy in your place of limbo and be content to know that He's got you covered! He loves your child even more than *you* do! He will never leave you nor forsake you, even if sometimes it feels as if He has. Remember, we are human, and just as our children are, we too are always doing the best we can at any given moment.

Psalm 34:18 states, "The Lord is close to the broken hearted; He rescues those who are crushed in spirit." Let him rescue you in this moment and bring you peace and contentment to a situation that doesn't feel very peaceful or content. Stay strong, stay the course. Don't become frazzled and try to do too much all at once. Slow down, listen for direction, and it will come. As surely as the dawn comes each morning, your answers will come. Isaiah 40:31 states, "They that wait upon the Lord shall renew their strength; they shall mount up with wings as eagles; they shall run and not be weary; and they shall walk and not faint." Wait upon the Lord, and he will give you strength and direction. God speed to you as you embark on your own personal journey.

Appendix A

Gluten-Free/Casein-Free Recipes

Below are a few of the recipes I created myself after much trial and error, and after learning how to use GF/CF flours with the help of Lisa Lewis, author of *Special Diets for Special Kids* (One and Two). I took the knowledge I learned from her cookbooks and created some recipes based on what Aaren ate at the time. It was my goal to make for a smooth transition as we entered the world of gluten-free/casein-free, so I took some of the recipes of the foods he was eating at the time and created a gluten-free/casein-free version in which he could not tell the difference! This was important at the time, because there was no fooling him into eating something he didn't want to eat, being as picky as he was then! I hope these recipes can be enjoyed by your children, and also that you can learn to make up your own favorites just as I have done, using the basic principles of working with gluten-free flours.

Chocolate Chip Cookies:

Ingredients:
- ½ cup fructose
- ½ cup brown sugar
- 1 cup Canola oil
- 2 eggs
- 1 tsp baking soda
- 1 tsp baking powder
- ½ tsp salt
- ¼ tsp Xanthum gum
- 1 ½ tsp vanilla extract
- 1 3-oz package GF/CF sugar free instant vanilla pudding mix
- ½–¾ cup finely chopped pecans (optional)
- 2 ½ cups Bob's Red Mill All Purpose Baking Flour
- ½ to 1 12 oz pkg of GF/CF chocolate chips (we used the Tropical Source brand)

Combine all and drop onto lightly greased cookie sheet in 1 tbsp portions. Bake at 350 degrees for twelve to fourteen minutes, depending on oven, and desired cookie consistency. I went more toward fourteen minutes to get a little crunchier cookie. Enjoy!

Pancakes:

**This batch makes plenty of pancakes so that you can freeze them and take them out to use as needed. They made a nice quick breakfast on busy mornings!

    4 eggs
    3 cups non-diary milk (we used Full Circle Vanilla Rice Milk)
    ¼ cup fructose (Xylitol, honey, or brown rice syrup can be used as well)
    ½ cup safflower oil
    1 tbsp baking powder
    1 tbsp baking soda
    4–5 cups GF/CF flour

Whisk eggs with milk together, add rest of ingredients. Mix well after each addition, and cook on skillet at 275 degrees until bubbly, then flip pancake for a minute or two longer, until lightly browned.

Banana Bread:

　　1/2 cup GF/CF margarine or shortening
　　2 ½ tbsp Stevia powder (plus enough almond meal to equal one cup)
　　2 eggs
　　½ tsp salt
　　1 tsp soda
　　1 tsp vanilla
　　2 tsp Xanthan gum
　　3 ripe bananas
　　½ cup dairy free milk (soy, rice, almond, etc)
　　2 cups GF/CF bean flour mixture (see below)
　　½ cup GF/CF chocolate chips

Cream shortening and sugar. Add eggs, salt, soda, and vanilla. Stir in bananas, milk, and then flour. Add chocolate chips. Bake at 350 degrees for forty-five to fifty minutes. Makes one large loaf or two smaller loaves.

Four Flour Bean Mix

2 cups Garfava bean flour
1 cup Sorghum flour
3 cups Cornstarch (or 1 cup Almond meal and 2 cups Cornstarch)
3 cups Tapioca flour
2 tsp Cream of Tartar

Mix all flours together, blend well. Store in airtight container in freezer for best results.

Pumpkin Bread:

2/3 cup shortening or GF/CF margarine
2 Tbsp Stevia powder (plus enough almond meal to equal 1 cup)
1 cup brown sugar
4 eggs
2 tsp soda
1 ½ tsp salt
1 ½ tsp baking powder
1 tsp cinnamon
½ tsp cloves
3 tsp Xanthan gum
2/3 cup water
2 cups canned pumpkin
2 ½ to 3 cups GF/CF flour (I used the Four Flour Bean Mix)

Mix and bake at 350 degrees for approx one hour. During last ten to fifteen minutes of baking, cover with large piece of tinfoil to prevent burning around edges. Let cool in pans for five to ten minutes, and then turn out onto waxed paper. Cover with large bowls to hold in moisture while cooling. Makes two large loaves.

Vanilla Chocolate Chip Muffins:

¾ cup canola oil (*or* ½ cup canola oil and ½ cup flaxseed, *or* ½ cup canola oil, ½ cup unsweetened applesauce)

3/4 cup brown sugar

2–3 Tbs white sugar for sprinkling

2 eggs

½ tsp salt

1 ½ tsp baking soda

1 ½ tsp baking powder

2 tsp vanilla

1 ½ tsp Xanthan gum

1 cup Very Vanilla Soy Milk (or other dairy-free milk)

½ cup GF/CF chocolate chips (extra chips for sprinkling on top of muffin, if desired)

2 cups GF/CF flour mixture

Combine ingredients in order listed, excluding white sugar for sprinkling, mixing well after each addition. Scoop batter into muffin pan and sprinkle tops of muffins with chocolate chips (I chopped them into bits) if desired. Bake for twenty to twenty-five minutes. Take out of oven and sprinkle each muffin with sugar. Lightly cover with tin foil to retain moisture while muffins are cooling. Remove from pan and store or enjoy.

Chocolate Muffin Version: Decrease vanilla to 1 tsp, add 2/3 cup baking cocoa, and decrease flour to 1 ½ cups.

Appendix B

Suggested Books and Websites

This is a short list of the books/sites available, but ones we found most helpful.

1. *Children with Starving Brains,* by Jacquelyn McCandless
2. *Enzymes for Autism and other Neurological Conditions,* by Karen DeFelice, http://www.enzymestuff.com.
3. *Son-Rise: A Miracle Continues,* by Barry Neil Kaufman, www.son-rise.org.
4. *Special Diets for Special Kids,* and *Special Diets for Special Kids II,* by Lisa Lewis, PhD.
5. *Asperger Syndrome and Difficult Moments: Practical Solutions for Tantrums, Rage, and Meltdowns,* written by Brenda Smith Myles and Jack Southwick.
6. *Turning Lead into Gold,* by Nancy Hallaway, and Zigurts Strauts.
7. *Amalgam Illness: Diagnosis and Treatment,* by Andrew Hall Cutler.
8. *Breaking the Vicious Cycle,* by Elaine Gottschall http://www.scdiet.com/.
9. *The Puzzle of Autism: Putting It All Together,* by Dr. Amy Yasko and Dr. Garry Gordon http://www.dramyyasko.com/Welcome.html.
10. *How to Compromise with Your School District without Compromising Your Child: A Field Guide for Getting Effective Services for Children with Special Needs,* by Gary Mayerson.

11. *Asperger Syndrome and Adolescence: Practical Solutions for School Success,* by Brenda Smith Myles and Diane Adreon.
12. *Incorporating Social Goals in the Classroom: A Guide for Teachers and Parents of Children with High Functioning Autism and Asperger Syndrome,* by Rebecca A Moyes.
13. *Social Skills Training for Adolescents with General Moderate Learning Difficulties,* by Ursala Cornish and Fiona Ross.
14. Gluten-Free/Casein-Free Info: http://www.gfcfdiet.com.
15. Direct Lab Services (Doctor's Data, Inc) (this includes the hair elements test), http://www.directlabs.com.
16. Chelation Overview (parent written, very good info, much more to explore on the site as well), http://www.danasview.net/chelate.htm.
17. TACA: Talk About Curing Autism, http://tacanow.com/default.htm
18. GENERATION RESCUE, http://www.generationrescue.org/.

    Generation Rescue is a Web site comprised of parents and mentor families, along with leading researchers and clinicians from around the world who have helped to discover and share the truth about potential causes of neurological disorders. This is one of the best resources I have found that effectively walks parents and/or caregivers through a step-by-step treatment plan for recovery. *Run—do not walk* to this Web site for valuable information on the biomedical treatment process, to read published science pertaining to autism—its causes, its treatments, etc.—to find a "Rescue Angel" in your city, to learn more about vaccinating safely, or to find a DAN! doctor in your area.
19. Children's Disability List of Lists: Find a listserv you can join, so that you can connect with other parents going through the types of things your family may be experiencing. http://www.comeunity.com/disability/speclists.html
20. Autism Research Institute: www.autism.com/index.asp.

21. Autism Society of MN: (look for a similar site in your state) http://www.ausm.org/autismInfo/documents/2007ResourceDirectory.pdf.

Suggested Sites for Supplements:

1. The Professional Supplement Center (free shipping!): https://www.professionalsupplementcenter.com.
2. Houston Enzymes: http://www.houston-enzymes.com.
3. Kirkman Labs: http://www.kirkmanlabs.com.
4. Brain Child Nutritionals: http://www.brainchildnutitionals.com.
5. Spectrum Supplements: http://www.spectrumsupplements.com.
6. VRP Vitamins: http://www.1to1vitamins.com.
7. The Vitamin Lady: http://www.vitaminlady.com.
8. Puritan's Pride Vitamins: http://www.puritan.com.

Appendix C

From the Heart

Special Moms

When a toddler gets into the plant pot dirt, a special mom appreciates how well their fingers work.

When a child yells, "NO!" a special mom enjoys the sound of their spoken word.

When a child must wear a helmet when riding a bike, a special mom is grateful that the helmet is not being worn to prevent injury from a seizure.

When a child plays the "chasing game" with mom in the grocery store, a special mom is thankful that her child can run at all.

When a child makes a mess while eating their lunch, a special mom is glad she does not have to put their lunch through a feeding tube.

When someone's child is having a "tantrum" in the shopping mall, a special mom never jumps to conclusions.

When a child gives themselves their first haircut, resulting in an embarrassing head shave, a special mom is blessed that they are not bald because they are going through chemotherapy.

When a child listens to annoying rap-music, a special mom enjoys that her child can hear any music.

When a child is at the hospital for an ear infection, a special mom feels blessed her child isn't in congestive heart failure ... again.

When a child complains about taking an awful-tasting cold medicine, a special mom is relieved that it is not heart medication, seizure medication, anti-rejections drugs, or something worse.

When a child in a wheelchair is out for a stroll with mom, a special mom understands that it may not be a good day to ask questions.

When a child needs extra tutoring to get through math, a special mom is relieved that her child doesn't need a team of seven people and five pieces of specialized equipment just to get him through the school day.

When a child needs the light on at bedtime, because they are scared of the dark, a special mom is thankful that her child does not live in constant darkness.

A special mom has learned to be less judgmental. A special mom's closest friends are other special moms.

A special mom looks at her special child with pride, while strangers often look at the special mom with pity.

A special mom appreciates all the things typical children do, whether naughty or nice.

A special mom always knows what not to say to another special mom.

A special mom rarely complains about the forty-five-minute wait at the doctor's office for a check-up, when she's spent months at a children's hospital with her dying child.

A special mom views the world through special eyes, ears, and hands.

—Luanna Buburuz

I'm Glad It's Not a Year Ago

Written by Diane Vrana, August 2005

Last year at this time (before Son-Rise and before biomedical treatment), my son, a nearly three-year-old boy, was completely non-verbal, would play repetitively for hours, screamed and banged his head for *hours* on end, and *could not leave the house* or tolerate anyone coming into our home. So much for a social life of *any* kind for *any* of us. So much for quality family time and everyday outings that others so unknowingly took for granted. What I wouldn't have given to simply be able to get my grocery shopping done during the day, rather than at 10:00 on a Friday night, while my son "slept" (I hoped!). So much for giving attention to our other two sons who so desperately needed it—we had too much to think about and do with Aaren. A year ago, none of us really had a "life." *I'm glad it's not a year ago ...*

One of us had to be with him at home at all times, and God forbid if *I* would be the one who would try to leave. Oh no, *out of the question* in his mind, for *me* to not be near him every second of every day. I would *sneak* out, only to hear his screams at my back as I walked away. I would call home several times while away, worried *sick* over him, but my husband usually couldn't even *get* to the phone, and if he *did*, we couldn't carry on a very long conversation, because my son would be screaming at the top of his lungs the entire time. I would *hide* in my bedroom or in the recesses of our basement, so that I could write out bills or check e-mails. Woe to the person who was left to watch him while I hid! I would *hurry* in the shower, because he didn't want me away from him and would bang his head on our tiled floor if he couldn't see me. My heart would race, my whole body tense and anxious, always trying to avoid another head-banging experience. A year ago, every day was a living nightmare, to say the least. *I'm glad it's not a year ago …*

He never slept consistently and would be up for hours at a time in the night. His naps were inconsistent in length, but oh how I *rejoiced* (and oftentimes collapsed myself!) when he *did* nap! Of course, not much of that time was "me" time, because my middle son was *starved* for attention and wanted me all to himself while Aaren was asleep. How could I refuse him? It's the least I could do, since the rest of my time *was* devoted to Aaren. Aaren received enemas every two days, because his constipation was so severe for so long. Hair cuts and fingernail trimmings were like wrestling matches—I holding him down, he fighting with all of his might, getting a kick, head butt, or scratch at my face any chance he could. He was simply *terrified* of such an experience! At the end of our "match," we would both have a few new bruises/cuts/scratches, with sweat streaming down our faces and tears on our cheeks. How *unfair* I would tell myself! Other mothers were painting their little girl's toenails or getting a "big boy hair cut" at the barber shop, while I was holding on for dear life to my son's hand or foot, trying so hard not to cut him with the clippers as he screamed and kicked at me. A year ago, those times were *unbearable … I'm glad it's not a year ago.*

A year ago, Aaren could not make eye contact for more than a few seconds, and even then it was usually only with me. When his dad would come home from work, our other boys would run to their dad with hugs and stories of the day, as typical children will do. Aaren would throw himself back on the floor and scream, all the while staring wildly at the ceiling, scooting himself backward until his head hit the wall. Welcome home, Dad. Every minute of every day was a struggle. I was emotionally and physically exhausted by 9:00 *am* (usually after a tantrum/crying fit before/through breakfast for what reason we generally did not know). I would say to myself, "Only eleven more hours, and I can put him to bed!" (Not that it mattered, because he was up half of the night, anyway!) Only eleven more hours of *attempting* to re-direct, of *attempting* to get him to play with one of his brothers, of *attempting* to stop him from banging his head on the wall in anger—*only eleven more hours*. A year ago, life was barely livable—life was not "life" to us, and was certainly nowhere near "normal." *I'm glad it's not a year ago …*

Just recently, Aaren "graduated" into the next level of swimming lessons with some candy and a "medal" he wore home proudly. This from a child who would not interact with anyone for any reason. He nearly *demanded* that he be allowed to attend his *own* swimming lessons after seeing his older brother at class! When I explained that it was his older brother's turn, he would say, *"Aaren's* turn!" When I said his older brother had his own teacher, Aaren would say, *"Aaren's* teacher! *Aaren* swim!" Needless to say, we signed him up the next night …

He *loved* his swimming instructor, Lindsy, and always gave her a warm welcome with a *"Hi, Lindsy!"* and a wave, and an enthusiastic *"Yea!"* when she would ask if he was ready to swim. He always left her at the end of class with hugs and kisses and a "See you later!" All he *talked* about was "teacher Lindsy." Did you notice how I said all he *talked* about—not just a little, mind you, a *lot!* Sort of like he *talks* and *talks* before bed. A year ago, *never* in my wildest dreams would I have ever thought I would have had to tell him to *stop talking!* It's a mixed blessing, to be sure, but boy *I am glad it's not a year ago!*

Libby is not the only teacher he loves. He also *loves* his speech therapist, Susan! He receives outside speech therapy twice a week, along with outside occupational therapy twice a week as well. Did you notice how I said *outside* speech and occupational therapy? Yes, we bring him to therapy. He waves good-bye to me in the waiting room, takes the hand of his therapist, and happily trots off to "work," telling them, "Mommy will be waiting for Aaren." The first time he did that, I just about fell on the floor! Tears unashamedly ran down my cheeks. *This,* I thought, coming from a child who a year ago, had the receptive language of a nine-month-old and the expressive language of a twelve-month-old. He has gained at least two and a half years of language in about ten months, and he is still gaining in both areas every day! Yes, Aaren, I thought, I will *always* wait for you—I'll *never* leave you! My heart is a flutter at the amazing gains he has made with his speech in the last year. When I hear him pray at night and use his words to say, "I love you, Jesus," *I am so glad it is not a year ago!*

A short while ago, he was down in his playroom for his two-hour session with a volunteer who he had just met the week before. I heard them singing, laughing, and playing with "ice cream" (play dough that he would scoop into bowls for each of them). He made up his own "green mint" song, as green mint is his favorite kind of ice cream. He then got silly and started calling vanilla "white mint." *Imagine* that—*imaginary* play from a boy who used to push cars around the room like a vacuum cleaner—a boy who used to "play" with colored blocks for hours, not building with them, necessarily, but sorting them into colors, rolling them, and certainly *not* letting anyone else *touch* them! Imaginary play from a boy who had no imagination whatsoever—who did not know *how* to play with toys, who simply stared off into space most of the time instead. Imagine *my son*, who could not tolerate another human being in his space—no eye contact, no physical contact, no language, *nothing*—was downstairs *without me* with a *new volunteer*, having a *great time*, and was being *completely social, flexible*, and *outgoing!* A year ago, my son didn't know the meaning of the word "social." *I'm glad it's not a year ago.*

Recently, I had to take him into the pediatrician's office for a quick visit. We brought along our "doctor's kit," and he had great fun "taking his temperature" and "giving himself a shot." He loved waiting in the waiting room and gazed excitedly at the fish swimming in the fish tank, saying, "Big fish, Mommy! *Huge* fish, Mommy! *Gigantic* fish!" Then he noticed the little fishes in the tank, and said, in a little squeaky voice, *"Tiny* fish, Mommy!" A year ago, he did not know what big or little meant, nor did he know what a fish was. He wasn't even aware that we had a dog in the house. Animals may have been pieces of furniture to him; he simply did not acknowledge their presence. When the nurse called his name, he went bounding into the hallway with her. He happily stepped onto the scale to see how much he weighed. He was a bit nervous when the doctor came in and talked to us, but when the doctor left, Aaren made sure he waved and said, "Bye-bye, doctor!"

A year ago, he would immediately fall to the ground once I got him out of the car *in the parking lot* before even getting *into* the doctor's office. I could barely sign him in at the registration desk, because he would be head-butting the counter and screaming bloody murder! Well-meaning nurses would come out to the waiting area and try to talk sweet and friendly to him. This only made matters worse. We were usually placed in a room *rather quickly* because we were a disturbance to the workers on the phones, and we were scaring the other kids in the waiting room. Once the doctor finally came in (forget about trying to weigh him or get his height—*not* going to happen!), he would scream so loudly that the doctor and I could hardly communicate at all. He would head butt me, hit at me, bite himself, whatever it took to get *out* of there. He was clearly scared to *death* and had *no idea* why we were there or even *where* we were. By the end of our visit, I would be sweating, crying (inside, at least), and carrying this struggling child back into the car—with new bruises on his head, with dirty looks coming at me in all directions for having such a *bratty* child, and with more screams coming from his mouth each time the car came to a stop during our ride home. (I never did really figure out why he would cry whenever we came to a stop.) *I'm so glad it's not a year ago.*

The progress we have made is *immeasurable* and worth every second of time spent in his playroom—every morsel of food he has consumed that is GF/CF. We are now completely off of the diet with the help of Houston Enzymes with more than excellent results! We have begun chelating with Authia cream (TTFD). The results have been amazing! I would have never dreamt my son would make up songs about ice cream or would run and play with his brother out in the backyard, pretending to be chased by "monsters" and loving every minute of it! I would never have dreamt that Aaren would initiate hugs and kisses with Grandma and Grandpa or aunties and uncles. After three years, Grandma finally got to hold her grandson in a loving embrace—for the first time. *Grandma is so glad it's not a year ago.*

Had we not stayed the course of Son-Rise and biomedical treatment, we would never have known the sense of *humor* my son has! We would never have *known* what he was thinking at any given moment. We would never have heard a spontaneous, "I love you, Mommy," or a well-deserved, "Thank you, Daddy." No, he is not completely recovered yet, and surely our life is not perfect! He still cries or tantrums from time to time, but now, he puts *himself* in time-out. He has a stubborn streak in him that is a mile long and insists on doing things *himself!* It is not always easy, and most tasks take lots of extra time, but he has *used* that stubborn independence to learn the age-appropriate things he so desperately needed to learn. He can now drink from a cup, open a door, bring his dishes to the counter after supper, name his colors, shapes, numbers, and letters—*use the potty*—things like that! He is doing so well that most people are shocked to hear he has autism. Several people have told me they never would have known had I not told them, and some still say they can't see it. *Not so* a year ago.

I thank God it's not a year ago …

References

1. McCandless J. (2003) *Children with Starving Brains: A Medical Treatment Guide for Autism Spectrum Disorder.* 2nd Edition. North Bergen, NJ: Bramble Books.

2. DeFelice, K. (2005) *Enzymes for Autism and Other Neurological Conditions: The Practical Guide for Digestive Enzymes and Better Behavior.* Johnston, IA: Thundersnow Interactive.

3. Wheeler, M. (2008) "An Introduction to Possible Biomedical Causes and Treatments for Autism Spectrum Disorders," Indiana Resource Center for Autism, http://www.iidc.indiana.edu/irca/Medical/Biomedical.html.

4. Kaufman, B. (1994) *Son-Rise, the Miracle Continues*, Tiburon, CA: H J Kramer Inc.

5. Wheeler, M, (2007) "Behavior and Inclusion on the Autism Spectrum." Conference, www.spectrumtrainingsystemsinc.com.

6. Kluth, P, (2007) "Behavior and Inclusion on the Autism Spectrum." Conference: www.spectrumtrainingstystemsinc.com.

7. Kanner, L. (1943) "Autistic Disturbances of Affective Contact", *Nervous Child 2* (1943): 217–250. Reprinted in *Childhood Psychosis: Initial Studies and New Insights*, ed. Leo Kanner (Washington, D.C.: V. H. Winston, 1973).

8. Wobus, J. (1993) "Autism Resources, FAQ." http://www.autism-resources.com/autismfaq-hist.html

9. Kanner, L . (1949). "Problems of Nosology and Psychodynamics in Early Childhood Autism". *Am J Orthopsychiatry* 19 (3): 416–26. PMID 8146742.

10. "Refrigerator Mother," Wikipedia, last edit, 2008 http://en.wikipedia.org/wiki/Refrigerator_mother.

11. Schnur, J. (2005) *Asperger Syndrome in Children*, American Academy of Nurse Practitioners, Provided by ProQuest LLC.

12. Cloud, H. and Townsend, J. (1998) *Boundaries with Kids: When to Say Yes, When to Say No to Help Your Children Gain Control of Their Lives* Grand Rapids, MI: Zondervan.

13. Kaplan, S. and Morris, J. (2000) "Kids at Risk." *US News & World Report* June 19, 2000, 47

14. Kennedy, Jr. R. (2005) "Deadly Immunity." *Rolling Stone Magazine*, June 20, 2005 http://www.rollingstone.com/politics/story/7395411/deadly_immunity/.

15. Connealy, L. (2006) "The Mad Hatter Syndrome: Mercury and Biological Toxicity." http://www.naturalnews.com/016544.html

16. Kurtz, S.—President (2008) "About Vaccines," Generation Rescue Web site, http://www.generationrescue.org/vaccines.html.

17. Miller, D. (2004) "A User Friendly Vaccination Schedule," Generation Rescue Web site, http://www.generationrescue.org/pdf/user_friendly.pdf.

18. Neustaedter, R. (2002) *The Vaccine Guide: Risks and Benefits for Children and Adults* Berkeley, CA: North Atlantic Books, Web site found at: http://www.cure-guide.com/Vaccine_Guide/Vaccine_Guide_excerpts/Homeopathic_vaccines/homeopathic_vaccines.html

19. Edelson, S. "The Candida Yeast-Autism Connection," Autism Research Institute. http://www.autism.com/triggers/candida_org.htm

20. Craft, D. "Symptoms of Yeast Overgrowth—Candida Albicans," Child Diagnostics, Inc. http://www.detoxmychild. org/yeast_overgrowth.htm

21. U.S. Dept. of Health and Human Services, NIH News, Feb. 2007, "Largest Ever Search for Autism Genes Reveals New Clues," http://www.nichd.nih.gov/news/releases/autism_gene_ reveals_clues.cfm.

22. U.S. Dept. of Health and Human Services, NIH News, Oct. 2006, "Gene Linked to Autism in Families with More Than One Affected Child," http://www.nichd.nih.gov/news/ releases/gene_linked_to_autism.cfm.

23. Wheeler, M. (2008) "An Introduction to Possible Biomedical Causes and Treatments for Autism Spectrum Disorders," Indiana Resource Center for Autism, http://www.iidc.indiana. edu/irca/Medical/Biomedical.html.

24. Rudy, L. (2007) "What is a Defeat Autism Now (DAN!) Doctor?" http://autism.about.com/od/alternativetreatmens/f/ dandoc.htm.

25. Novella, S. (2007) "Vaccines and Autism: Myths and Misconceptions," *Skeptical Inquirer Magazine* : Nov/Dec 2007, http://csicop.org/si/2007-06/novella.html.

26. Lewis, L (2006) "What is Celiac Disease and the Gluten-Free Diet?" Celiac Website, http://www.enabling.org/ia/celiac/ index.html#deff.

27. Remelin, R (2004) "Dr. Boyd Haley Exposes the Phony Science on Amalgam Safety," The Last Outpost, http://52. thelastoutpost.com/video-1/health/dr-boyd-haley-on-mercury- toxicity-and-autism.html.

28. Moore, Beth (1998) *Living Beyond Yourself: Exploring the Fruit of the Spirit* Nashville, TN: LifeWay Press

29. Moore, Beth (2002) *Believing God,* Nashville, TN: LifeWay Press